The Dude, the Ducks
and Other Tales

Kathi — You may
identify with some
of these stories because
I see Jesus - joy in
you!

Joy Olmstead

# The Dude,

# the Ducks

## and Other Tales

*Insights from Life in the Country*

# *Lois Olmstead*

**CHRISTIAN PUBLICATIONS, INC.**
CAMP HILL, PENNSYLVANIA

## CHRISTIAN PUBLICATIONS, INC.

3825 Hartzdale Drive, Camp Hill, PA 17011
www.christianpublications.com

*The Dude, the Ducks
and Other Tales*
ISBN: 0-88965-200-7

LOC Control Number: 2001-135747

© 2002 by Lois Olmstead

Printed in the United States of America

02  03  04  05  06      6  5  4  3  2

This book is dedicated to

**Bud and Lorraine Bohleen**

my mom and dad

who gave me the foundation for a life of joyful adventure
by loving me, each other and our Lord Jesus Christ.

They have let me be the "hired hand"
even when they didn't need one.

For my dad, who still tells me how to drive,
and my mom, who still tells me to get plenty of rest—
I love you, and I trust you will see that love in these memories.

# Contents

*Jesus said, "I am come that they might have life,
and that they might have it more abundantly" (John 10:10, KJV).*

# CHAPTER 1

# Ranch Girl
# Goes Home

*Most favorite of all the pieces of this columnist were the ones when I went home to "help" my folks. You will love meeting my mom and dad. I praise God for allowing me to be born in this family.*

This week, I realized a special blessing. This blessing is the ability to turn into a kid again. Turning into a kid again at my age is quite an accomplishment. I do it by going home. By "going home" I mean going back to the ranch in the Shields Valley near Livingston, Montana (sixty miles from Yellowstone National Park), where I was raised and where my parents are still active ranchers. Robert and I love going for a visit. My parents tell their friends, "The kids are here!"

"Get your boots and hat," my mom said the minute I arrived. "We have to feed a jag of hay." I got my old jeans and a sweatshirt. I was pulling on my boots when she honked a few minutes later. I jumped into the old orange Dodge truck during takeoff. I managed to get in without being dragged underneath. We raced over the snowbanks and two ditches and swung around my dad in the tractor to get the gate in front of him.

"I'll get the gate," I said to no one. My mom was already out of the truck and had the gate open. She swung back in behind the wheel. Dad was yelling something to us as he drove by. We both nodded, but of course neither understood what he had yelled. We raced on to the next gate.

"Get the gate," my mom said. "I'll drive up to the hay corral. Keep those cows from getting out. . . ." she hollered out the window at me as she drove off. As I stood waiting for Dad, I thought, *I should write a book on gates. That has been my expertise since I was ten. And not one gate opens the same way. I think inventors must spend years trying to come up with creative, magical ways to latch ranch gates!* I quit talking to myself and yelled at two cows coming my way, then yelled at Dad as he went tearing through the gate, "Don't hit the cows. . . ." My next two thoughts were *Why does everything on this ranch have to be done in a hurry?* and *I suppose I don't have to tell him not to hit the cows!*

While he loaded a big round bale onto the rod at the back of the tractor and then drove down into the pasture with the cows and calves looking like teenage boys at the lunch line, Mom showed up. Dad came back, hollering something to us from inside the cab on the tractor. Cabs are a wonderful modern addition to tractors, keeping out the heat and the dust, and on a day like today, the bitter-cold wind. "What'd he say?" I asked.

"I don't know. I never know," Mom laughed. "I can't hear a word he says when I've got my hat on. I just try to read his mind." At the barn he told us he was going to feed a bale of straw in the one corral. Then we were going to cut two cows out. (That means separating them from the rest of the herd.)

"Didn't he just tell us that at the house?" I asked Mom.

"Yup. And that was what he just hollered to us from the tractor. He says he always had to tell you kids everything three times in order for you to get the job done right! Now he just does it from force of habit!" We went back to the house.

"We've got to hustle," Dad said. He put a log in the stove and grabbed his hat. "You drive your pickup," he told me with a grin. "We'll save our gas." Mom got in the middle and Dad jumped in. "Now don't hit my tractor as you back out." We were on our way to town for coffee with friends. (Another change in ranching I noted: town used to be much farther from the ranch than it is today!) As we neared the Trail Rite Inn, Dad said, "Get in the right lane and slow down."

Mom said, "Just follow that yellow truck. You have to slow down and then turn right at the stop sign."

Dad said, "Just go in the first turn. Park by that brown truck." By then we were all laughing.

"Here is what you do, Lois: If we both tell you the same thing, then do it," laughed my mom.

"OK," I said. Me, the dude, the kid.

I held my pen poised over the contest form at Rimrock Mall. The entry blank said, "Tell why your mom should be Queen for a Day at Rimrock Mall."

My mom has been a Montana ranch wife for over fifty years. She and Dad raised my brother and me with hard work, discipline and lots of love. And we had fun too. My mom raised chickens and had a big garden. As I got older I realized that she didn't do this for fun; it was our groceries. She still gardens. My family gets jars of Gram's delicious fruits and vegetables in the fall. People always think she's my sister when they meet us together because she looks so young. (I tell her that is great for her, but I sure must be aging fast!) She tells me, "You are only as old as you feel." She looks great when she is all dressed up for church or dinner out with Dad. But the minute she gets home, she jumps into her Levis and boots. She looks great then too.

She can cook a delicious meal when ten people pop in unexpectedly. She told me the guest bed had been occupied thirty-seven nights in a row during hunting season by different visitors. I guess that is what motivated her to build a log guest cabin out behind the house. She peeled the logs, used the tractor and a forklift to lift them in place and even built the bunk beds and the outhouse (with a half-moon in the door to make it authentic).

5

My pen is still poised midair over the entry blank. My mom drives the hay baler and leads a Bible study. My mom floats the Yellowstone River and vaccinates the calves. My mom can change a tire or pull a calf. She has shot deer, antelope, elk and moose. A black bear she saw is now a rug hanging in their log home which she and Dad designed. She went on a eighty-mile trail ride in the Teton Mountains a few years ago, slept on the ground and loved it. When I called her on her birthday last Sunday, she told me she had planted 250 baby Christmas trees the day before.

She laughingly told me about being out marking the new calves when an upset mom cow took after her and Dad. She had gotten off her three-wheeler a few minutes before. So Dad took a belly dive onto the hay wagon and Mom scaled the pigpen fence in one leap. Thankfully no pigs were there.

The entry blank is still blank.

What I appreciate most about Mom is her example of being a wife and a mother. Her faith in God through the good times and the bad has inspired my own faith.

I wipe a few tears from my eyes and crumple up the entry blank with a smile. My mom can't be Rimrock Mall's Queen for a Day. She hasn't got time.

Happy Mother's Day, Mom. I love you.

When my dad read the column about my mom, he said, "That was great. Now just don't get any ideas about Father's Day!"

Dear Dad: You know how difficult it has always been for me to follow your instructions. I remember how you'd give me directions for chores. You would tell me to give two flakes of hay to the horses, feed a bucket of grain to the 4-H calves and bring in three loads of wood.

You would repeat it twice while I was getting my coat. Then I would race out to the barn, give the horses two buckets of grain, feed the calves three flakes of hay and bring in one load of wood. I should have listened.

I remember when you told me not to drive the old Plymouth because it didn't have brakes. But when Mom told me to get a jug of milk from the neighbors, I jumped into the Plymouth and zoomed over the hill. Going down the first hill I remembered what you had said, but it was too late. I drove like Mario Andretti over the hills and around the corners right into the Evanses' yard. I thought the only way to stop was to aim at something bigger than the car, so I headed for their barn. I only knocked out three cinder blocks. I jumped out of the car and looked toward home. I could see the cloud of dust billowing like a hurricane down our road. You made it in record time. I am sure you thought I was killed. I should have listened.

I was eight when you taught me to drive on the little Ford tractor. I guess I always had a heavy foot because I never left the house without ten minutes of driving instructions. (Even last week when I went to Wyoming to speak, you called to tell me how to drive. That was ten minutes long distance.)

I remember when I was driving from Billings to Livingston to teach sewing lessons. I had coffee with you one night before I drove the 100 miles back home. "Now, there's lots of deer on the road by Big Timber, so you drive slow!" you said.

I should have listened. A highway patrol pulled me over for speeding. When he came up to the car, I said, "Drats! My dad told me to watch out for deer. He didn't say a thing about patrolmen!" He didn't crack a smile as he wrote out my ticket. I thought you'd never find out. But you went to Big Timber to get your hair cut (they still charged $1) and read it in their paper!

I think you lost most of your hair when I started to date. You told me where I could go and when. You checked on the boys' driving. You told me what time to be in and not to "park" in the yard after I got home. I didn't listen. You reminded me by blinking the yard light. I wasn't too worried about one blink, but three blinks meant my date had overextended his welcome.

You were very strict. And I certainly got a goodly number of educational lessons applied to my backside when I was young. (I still think I got more than Ron did!) However, strict as you were, I never had a single doubt about your immense love for us kids. You always let us know how much you loved us.

You taught us most by example. I think I was about ten when you and Mom gave your lives to the Lord. And every night before you went to bed, you knelt by that white footstool in the living room and prayed. Every morning, I would see you reading your Bible before you went out for chores. You taught me that living for the Lord was a daily walk, not just a Sunday affair.

When I went to college, I knew you were praying for me. After I got married, I knew you were praying for the two of us. Today, when you are busier and working harder than ever on the ranch, I know you are praying for our children, their wives and families, and us too.

I know you told me not to write about you in the paper. I should have listened . . . ?

Happy Father's Day, Dad. I love you.

I tell my friends I am going to the ranch "to help my folks." That could be stretching the truth. I think I go to entertain—I doubt I'm much help! The last trip I met a dangerous enemy. A new gate.

It was a gate suitable for dangerous prison inmates rather than mere cows. It had a two-inch strap of iron bent in a circle fastened to the fence post. That fastened to an iron apparatus that included a taut spring and a slot for a straight piece of iron to rest in when the gate was closed. To hold this iron bar in place, it was necessary to slide a bolt through a hole.

On the first day in a freezing, howling Livingston wind, my dad jumped off the tractor and opened the gate. I watched as he pulled out the bolt, letting the ring of iron slide off the gate post and then opened the gate wide for the tractor to go through.

So when he approached it later—"I'll get the gate!" I hollered over the wind and the noise of the tractor as he drove through. It was a struggle. You really needed three arms to get this gate closed. God forgot and only gave me two. By bracing my leg against the gate pole when it got somewhat vertically lined up with the fence post and using a hammerlock on the top with my right arm, I used every ounce of strength in me to wrestle the iron ring over the post. Somehow I managed to get the iron bar into its slot. With a desperate prayer, I held onto the iron bar with one hand and slid the bolt into place. I stepped back. The gate stood. The iron bar was latched.

"That's the best gate on the place," my dad said later. "It stretches the gate good and tight. It's secure."

"Is there gate school somewhere?" I asked. "How do they come up with all these different mind-boggling latches?"

"Everyone just keeps thinking they can make a better one."

Well, now you will learn why I am the ranch "dude." The next day we went out to do the same thing we did the day before . . . the same thing my folks have been doing twice a day all winter. The only variants are how cold the wind was, how deep the snow was and how successful the mom cows were at giving birth without help. When we got to *the* gate, I jumped out of the pickup. "I can get it," I said confidently.

I knew what I had to do to unlatch the gate. Just pull the bolt out of the hole. The bolt that held the bar of iron hooked to the round iron circle that was over the gate post. I pulled out that bolt—and screamed!

That iron bar flipped up like it was hooked to a bomb. The spring that held the iron circle made a *whoosh* sound as it flew past my nose. In less then two seconds the before-taut gate was lying like a snake at my feet. I touched my nose with my gloved hand just to make sure it was still there.

My mom was in the pickup. When I got in, she said, "I knew that was going to happen. I knew it, but I just couldn't get the window rolled down fast enough to yell. Are you all right?"

"Yup—and I am now wide awake too." By then I was laughing. Fear does that to me. I was still laughing when we caught up to Dad. "You ought to harness the power in that thing," I said to him. "You could energize an electric fence with the power in it!"

"You've got to be smarter than the gate," he said to me with a grin.

"Don't go there," I retorted.

Me, the ranch hand.

No—me, the dude. The entertainer.

"I guess you couldn't use a five-day planner in your line of work," I said to my mom as our old blue truck bounced along a narrow road paved with mud and snow and hemmed by a barbed wire fence. This is our second annual Lois-goes-home-to-help-with-calving trip. I had packed a bag with old cowboy clothes and lots of winter wear and headed west with the blessing of He-who-married me.

The first night we had one new calf when we checked at 10:30 p.m., which is one hour past my bedtime. I slept through the next two calls at 2:30 and 5:30 a.m. I did manage to get up in time for breakfast.

**Day One:** After two pots of coffee around the woodstove and a precious prayer time together, we have breakfast. Dad makes the toast. (No one can make toast as good as my dad can make it.) Mom cooks oatmeal, sets the table and puts out grapefruit and juice. I get dressed. Only because I am the daughter do I get to wear my sleeping clothes after the sun comes up.

(No, wait. Before this, we weren't going to fix breakfast because we are going to Big Timber to get a tub of mineral. We'll have breakfast at Frye's Café. "We haven't been there in ages," Dad says. He calls the mineral guy. "Nope, don't have any. I am out. My truck is stuck in eastern Montana with the roads closed. I will call you when my truck gets through.")

So then, breakfast. Then we get our winter duds on and go out to the corrals. We have a new calf from one of the heifers we cut out the day before. Mom and I said she wouldn't calve for days, but Dad yelled, "In," when we were cutting them out. (Good thing.)

Mom was the *In* and I was the *Out* gate. If you haven't been on a ranch, you would not have any idea of the importance of being a gate person. It comes fraught with risks. If you mess up, you make yourself liable for . . . well, I won't go there, except to say it adds a considerable amount of time to fix your mistake. Suffice it to say I *have* been there and I know what I am talking about.

We run the heifer and her calf into the straw-filled recovery room in the barn. "Good little bull calf," Dad says as he takes a square chunk out of the newborn's ear with the earmarker. The calf doesn't even wince. He is still getting adjusted to the temperature change in his atmosphere. It is 18 degrees above zero this morning with an east wind.

Next, Mom gets a flake of hay while Dad carries a five-gallon bucket down to the creek for water. A much older calf that had a broken leg is in a small pen. The cast is off now, but he still doesn't want to use the leg. Somebody's loose dogs chased this calf until it fell and broke its hind leg, which is a whole 'nother story. We check out the leg and decide a shot of penicillin is needed. Mom and I jump into the truck and head for the house.

I just wish you could see me. I can get the door open and have one foot on the ground before the pickup comes to a complete stop. I have figured out the gate latch (one of forty-two different types of fastening inventions, which we have discussed before) and can open the gate, swing it back without falling on the ice, shut the gate and jump back into the pickup quicker than you can pour a cup of coffee. Speaking of which, it is now 10 a.m. and the dude thinks she might miss her 10 o'clock coffee this morning. We will be fortunate to make it back to the house in time for lunch. So much for my daily planner schedule. The rest of the day goes by in a blur.

**Day Two:** It is Sunday, the only day you will see boxes of cold cereal on the table for breakfast at the ranch. We have prayer time around the woodstove, Dad makes the toast and then we eat a quick breakfast with lots of friendly guessing and discussion on which cow had a calf last night. On with our outdoor clothes. Mom wears a pair of brown Carhartt insulated coveralls we're going to donate to the Smithsonian Institute when she goes to heaven. They are full of holes. The daughter, the dude, tells her she looks like a bag lady.

She says, "When these coveralls wear out, I am quitting this job." That is a vain threat we have heard from this ranch hand before. The head of the outfit dresses worse. His brown Carhartt coat has the red lining peeking through tattered threads at the elbows.

He buckles on leather chaps and black overshoes to protect his boots and add warmth for his feet. The dude puts on two pairs of pants, two pairs of knee socks (fashionably purple), a pink turtleneck, a red flannel shirt from Robert's side of the closet at home and an orange sweatshirt. Opening the closet door of the mudroom at the ranch, she gets the hand-me-down red and blue ski jacket that was left at the ranch by one of her boys years ago. Yellow mud boots and a white and purple ski hat finish the ensemble of the dude.

The garage door whirrs up as Dad starts the four-wheeler, the modern horse of today's rancher. Mom starts the little battered blue pickup which has been plugged in all night so it would start. The dude opens the steel gate by the house (hook latch) and jumps into the pickup after they both go through. The next gate, a quarter-mile down a dirt road, is her next. Another hook latch, but while it is being opened, one must make sure no yearlings run through the gate.

Yearlings act like adolescents—no sense. It is a wonder they can gain the weight that will insure a profit the next fall. They run to the feeder filled twice daily with hay. They run to the black plastic tubs filled with Crystalyx, a mineral to build body weight. Then they run to the creek to drink. They are always at the gates, waiting to dash through, the epitome of "grass is always greener on the other side of the fence."

Dad started buying yearlings the year before in December. The profit in raising yearlings comes from the amount of gain on the animals by the time they are sold in the fall. He bought 100 head the first year and wanted more. Mom and I kept telling him that was enough. It was a venture not without risk and a lot of money invested. Finally we convinced him to stop at 100. That fall, after a good year of grass due to lots of rain, he sold the yearlings. No one at the shipping yard could believe the amount of gain he got on those yearlings. (Mom and I did notice he talked to the yearlings a lot. We were talking to God about his talking to them!) Dad called me that night with the weights and the price per pound. He had done very well. "Mom and I told you you should have bought more!" I told him. This year we didn't offer any suggestions as he bought another bunch of yearlings.

Another quarter-mile and we arrive at the barn. First priority is to check the first corral with the heifers. First-time mothers often require birthing assistance. Some are eating at the feeder we filled with hay yesterday. Others stand around the gate that leads down to the creek, waiting. Since opening gates is the job of the daughter-dude, she walks through the heifers and opens the gate. This is a wire over a nail on a wood gate with a twine tie looped through the boards of the gate for insurance. Then she steps out of the way quick because the mob has no consideration even for the female in yellow boots and purple hat.

Next the brown iron gate is opened (a pipe connected to a smaller pipe that goes through a hole in a flat piece of metal in the corral fence) and closed so the "drop bunch" won't go in the alleyway. The yellow boots are picking up a brown tone as she walks down a hill past the feeder in this corral. A wire gate with a wire hoop over the gatepost is a tough one. You have to muscle up to the gate, put the gatepost in your armpit and use all the Cheerios in your system to pull the gate up, sliding the loop off. This gate is then hooked in a similar fashion along the corral. Each night this gate has to be closed so that one of the cows will not mistake the creek for a birthing room. The "drop bunch" is a group of cows that have been cut out (more gate work) from the main herd because they will (seemingly) be calving soon. Any woman, obstetrician or vet knows that the birthing time of a pregnant being is predictable—with an element of error.

This day we find a new calf shivering out in the field near its mom-cow. Mom-cow had not made the cut into the drop bunch but that did not stop her from having her baby. Fortunately, the birth was just an hour before, so the calf will make it, not suffering too much from the below-zero temperature of its delivery day. Dad loops a rope that is tied on the four-wheeler around the hind legs of the calf and slowly drags it to the barn. It is a slow trip of stopping and starting. He goes forward a few feet, than stops and waits for the cow to follow. A good mom-cow will follow closely. An "old rip" will just stand and watch its calf being towed away.

This mom-cow gets a mother-of-the-year award. Not only does she follow closely, but she wants to eat the rope, the four-wheeler, the blue pickup and the people involved. The daughter jumps out of the pickup as soon as the entourage gets close to the barn. The gate (a pipe latch thing) is thrown open as well as the gate (a board that slides into a square space notched out of the barn door) to the calving shed. It is hard to get both gates open when you feel like a rodeo clown fighting off Bodacious. If all works well (sometimes it does, sometimes it doesn't), the cow and calf are now in cow-heaven: a warm barn with clean straw and privacy. A place to celebrate birth. A place to see if the feeding mechanisms work. A place to see if the mom-cow and baby calf know what comes next—eating, growing, bonding.

It seems that is what the outfit boss (the dad), the top hand (the mom) and the daughter (the dude) are doing. Bonding. We don't have time to think about that. We race to the house where showers and different duds transform the crew into churchgoers and we head for town.

**Day Three**: I was barely asleep when Dad knocked on my bedroom door. It was midnight and dark. We drove a mile through the fields to the orchard to check the cows. I followed Dad as he walked through the 150 cows, checking for newborn calves or cows showing signs of giving birth soon.

"Over here," he hollered. The anxious mother stood by her calf. The calf was wet and already had frost on its curly black hair. Our breath came in clouds as Mom drove the pickup close to the calf. Dad let the cow get a good whiff of her calf and then lifted the calf into the back of the pickup. "If you don't let that cow get a good whiff of that calf, she won't know it is hers and then you've got real problems," my mom explained when I hopped into the warm cab of the pickup. She drove slowly toward the barn with Dad holding the calf on the tailgate and the cow anxiously following. I opened the gates. They had built a small room in a corner of the barn. It had fresh straw and a heat lamp in it.

Dad let the cow sniff the calf again and then closed the door on the "calf-ink-a-bator."

"We got there just in time," my dad said. We checked two other corrals of cows. "Everything looks OK for now," he said. We headed home where a glance at the thermometer showed -21 degrees F.

I got my nightgown on and crawled in bed. It seemed like only minutes had passed before I heard, "Lois, time to check the cows." We repeated the procedure. One more calf. He went in the little heated room also. When we got home I fell asleep as soon as my head hit the pillow. But there was more for the dude to learn.

After breakfast and devotions, we got ready to feed. I looked like the Abominable Snowman. Mom and I in the pickup followed Dad on the tractor. I opened and shut gates. Dad loaded a 1,200-pound round bale of straw onto the pickup and carried two on the tractor. We went from the field to the orchard to the corral, feeding the cows and the bulls. Another trip to the haystack brought breakfast to the heifers.

Dad said, "Drive up to the orchard and get 14."

I thought we'd be herding fourteen cows down to the barn. But I soon caught on—the cows have ear tags with numbers. We cut out Number 14 and headed her to the barn. I was ready for a coffee break and a nap. But that had to wait.

We put 14 in a pen with fresh straw. Her water bag was protruding under her tail. She would have a calf soon. "We'll check her right after lunch," Dad said as we drove back to the house. I opened and closed the gates. I could not believe how tired I was. *And they do this every day*! I thought to myself. I resolved to check the labels on the vitamins they take each day.

We went back to the barn after lunch. Number 14 had had her calf. "That calf has not sucked," Dad said to my mom. "You better fix a bottle."

I was still trying to figure out how he could tell when Mom hollered for me to "get the gate and get in on the double." I did remember from my childhood that all things on the ranch were done "on the double!"

Cow 14 had a nitwit calf. It would not suck. We put the cow in the chute and tried to teach the calf that breakfast was available. But the calf couldn't or wouldn't understand. So Dad milked the cow, who was not used to being milked and let us know she did not like the idea by kicking and bellowing. Mom fed the calf with a bottle.

We checked the cows every two hours. Each time we'd spot a cow that was about to calve, we put her in the corral by the barn. I thought that was quite an accomplishment considering we were looking through blowing snow in the dark of night at black cows with a flashlight. To be totally honest, I do have to admit we ran #113 into the shed on my advice and she still hasn't calved at last report!

I really do not know how my folks keep up this pace. I won't tell you their ages, but they are old enough to have had me, and they can run circles around me.

We had twenty-six new babies. We had lost one. That night Dad and I checked cows at 10:30 p.m. while Mom fed 14's calf. Dad said, "We will go again at midnight."

The long nights and hard work were taking their toll. It was a record cold spell and just getting around with all those duds took effort. We overslept by an hour. Dad checked one corral and I walked through the other. I saw a calf lying in the snow and was relieved to see it was still breathing, even though covered with snow and ice. I grabbed a foot and pulled the calf toward the barn with the mom-cow right behind me. I was too afraid to stop for her to get a whiff. I just pulled. We rubbed the calf down and put it under the heat lamp on clean straw. It bellowed for its mom. I felt like an EMT. Lifesaver to the rescue.

We went back to the house and hit the bed. I no longer undressed. I just fell on the bed and went to sleep. Dad woke at 3 a.m. and we made the rounds again. The calf I had "rescued" was dead. Dad told me we could not keep saying, "If only . . ."

**Day Four:** The thermometer dipped to 32 below. We moved the entire herd of cows down to the barn and spread precious bales of straw for bedding. Dad fed additional hay. Cow 14's calf was getting weak. It wouldn't drink from the bottle. We put 14 in the chute again and had another unsuccessful feeding lesson. "We have to tube him," my mother said. I watched as she poured some of the cow's milk into a bottle with a long plastic tube attached. Dad held the calf and Mom tried to force the tube down the calf's throat.

The calf bellowed and the jealous mother-cow charged. Mom hit the fence and banged her head against the post.

My dad said, "Lois, get in here and stand between us and the cow!" I thought that was a very dangerous place for a dude. But the daughter said, "Yes, Dad," praying every step of the way.

We went back to the house, and during a brief nap, I dreamed my house was full of zoo animals and the Colstrip Fire Department had to come break windows so the giraffes and tigers could get out. "I think I need to go home," I told my dad. "I think I am getting a little too involved."

Two days later, our prayers and Mom's persistence paid off. She came back from the barn to report that 14's calf had sucked. Now we could turn them out into the nursery field. I'll tell you about the field names later. (That was one of the dude's brilliant ideas.)

## CHAPTER 2

# They Keep Letting
# the Dude Return

If you aren't from rural background, you might think March is just the month you have to round up all your checks and stuff for income tax time. In the cattle business, March is calving month. Which has much to do with income also. Getting each cow to have a healthy calf figures greatly (hopefully) in your income for the year. It is generous and loving of ranch folks to allow a "dude" on their place during this critical phase of their yearly operation. However, when the dude is the daughter, allowances are made.

"When do I get to have brown clothes?" the daughter asked the father, the head of the cattle outfit. This question came after a scene in the corral.

A hostile mom-cow was being herded into the calving shed. When said cow saw the dude outfitted in her blue and red ski jacket ensemble with a pink and purple stocking cap, newly purchased pink ski gloves (guaranteed for below zero weather) and yellow mud boots, she went wild. The fashion plate was told to exit out the rear door before the cow scaled the nearest gate. After the cow-soon-to-give-birth (if she didn't change her mind after this episode) was safely in the barn, it was explained that pregnant cows are quite temperamental. They react violently to strangers.

"Well, if you would just let me wear some brown clothes, I wouldn't stand out so much!" the daughter said.

"When you've been here forty years, you can have some brown clothes too," the head cowman said.

"That's certainly something to look forward to," the daughter retorted. There wasn't much time for any further discussion. The maternity ward was strained to the max. It had started to snow and the strong wind was from the east.

"A change in weather always brings on the calves," said the wife-mother-top-hand. Top-hand does not carry any status or an inflated paycheck. It just means you are married to the boss and have a pair of brown coveralls.

Besides the heifer pen, the drop corral and sick bay, the cattle operation has a calving shed. This has partitions so more than one cow or cow-calf pair can be kept in. Also in the calving shed, there is a very small wooden enclosure that is equipped with a heat lamp. It is the size of a doghouse. This is like a calf-incubator—or as I called it, Calf Intensive Care. It doesn't take very long for a wet newborn calf to chill. A few hours in ICU can save the calf's life. Another small area, the size of a small bedroom, is Calf Constant Care. It has no heat lamp but with fresh straw, a roof and walls, is out of the wind.

Then there is the Psychiatric Ward. This is not a pleasant place. It has high board fences. A chute snaps shut with a spring release when the cow's head goes through the opening. Kicking your offspring every time it tries to eat or not feeding your baby at all are reasons to get admitted here. Please note that all these place names are given by the dude. The rancher calls them all "the pen."

How one is to distinguish "the pen" from "the other pen" remains a mystery to me. Hence the names. (I doubt the names will stick when I leave.)

A big black Angus cow with a #67 ear tag was in the Psychiatric Ward. She deserved to be there. Rather than feed her offspring of the day before, she kicked it and refused to let it suck. She became a more willing mother when her head was caught in the stocks. A small gate was open and her baby was pushed into position near the feeding tubes. The pair spent the night in the small enclosure. By morning it was evident that the calf had partaken of breakfast and the rebel was ready to be a mother.

"It's time to let them out," said the rancher. He pushed the heifers in the corral outside the calving shed down the alleyway to the creek and shut that gate. The wife-cowhand stood at the corral gate ready to let #67 and her offspring out into the sheltered creekside field designated "The Nursery" by the dude. This field held all the mom-cows and their calves.

"Yikes," yelled the daughter-dude, who was at the calving shed gate. "HELP!" Old #67 decided she wanted out *now*. She had two feet over the gate, head rearing and bellowing wildly. "Get down, you old bat," yelled the daughter with faked bravado. "STOP!" A panic prayer was sent to her Heavenly Father.

"Let her go. Open the gate!" yelled my earthly father.

"Yeah, right!" I slipped the board out of the latch and ran for my life. Old 67 went by me like a tornado with her calf at her heels.

"Now do I get brown clothes?" I asked my dad as we sat around the woodstove in the living room having a cup of coffee.

"I'll think about it," he said. "I'll think about it."

"I thought you'd be taking it a little easier now," I said to Mom. I had stopped at the ranch for the weekend after helping with a marriage seminar in Bozeman. I knew most of the calving was done and the weather was nicer. Of course I know there is the branding and then moving the cattle to the pasture. Then it's time to begin all the ground work: drilling, seeding, ditch work and then fence repair and irrigating before it's time to bale hay. I had ranch clothes I'd left there, so I jumped in with Mom when they started their day after our coffee and a very special prayer time.

"Well, it's rained for several days. That is conducive to illness in the new babies," she said as she maneuvered the pickup close to Dad's four-wheeler. Dad hollered, "Get that tube of stuff out of the front of the pickup."

"While you're there," Mom added, "bring another bottle of penicillin." I did both. "Now get the air out of the needle, put it in the bottle, draw it up to the line," she instructed. "Now jam it right here." I did it! All this time the mother cow is pawing, snorting and breathing down my neck. I tried to remember what the rodeo clowns do but my fear was causing a blank brain. We got back to the house at noon. That was just morning chores.

"This ranch work," I said to my parents wisely, "is never over till it's over, is it?"

They agreed. Maybe the dude was catching on.

It is quite a deal when three weeks of columns can be written by the dude-also-weekly-columnist, in exchange for one week at the ranch of her parents!

I was thinking . . . *Maybe they could start a side business. Like those working vacations on a real cattle ranch that you see advertised in magazines. Having experienced writer's block on more than one occasion, I am sure writers would gladly pay a sum to go to a place where material for columns is readily available. I'd better suggest that idea to my dad.*

"You mean to tell me that I would have dudes come stay with us a week to get stuff to write about?" he asked.

"Oh, yes, I'm sure it would work," I said. "It would be grand. They could stay in the cabin. That ought to be worth several writing ideas right away. Then they could help you do feeding, fencing and calving. People would pay to do that so they could break through their writing blocks. Other people would come and spend a week just like I did and help just like I did," I said.

"Just like you did?"

"Yup," I said, feeling downright smart.

"*Just* like you did?" he said again.

"Yup."

"Well, in that case, I would have to say no. That just wouldn't work."

"Why not?"

"Because—correct me if I'm wrong—you were here five days. We went out for breakfast twice. We met friends or family for lunch three times. We went out to supper twice. You and your mother went shopping in Bozeman for a whole afternoon." He paused. "I'd have to get a pencil to figure the cost of the meals, plus you took my top hand off to visit three times!"

"Oh, it wouldn't be like that. I had to visit everybody. These people would be there to help."

"Just like you?"

"Yup."

"This ranch can't afford that kind of help. We have to make a living here, you know."

"Just think how good I was at opening all those gates. . . ."

"Yes, and if your nose was a quarter inch longer, you would have cut it off when you opened that one gate! Think what that would have cost me."

I was beginning to get the point. OK, so it would not be a smart money move for them. Just the same, it was a good idea! "I get the picture. But we sure did have some good laughs, didn't we?"

"Without a doubt," he said. "I just don't know if we could find anyone to provide that amount of entertainment."

I let that one slide. I was thinking about the morning at the barn when I had taken along our video camera to capture their morning routine to show the grandkids and great-grandkids. "Here we are in the pickup, heading up to the barn to check for calves," I narrated as Mom and I bounced along in the old Dodge pickup. (In the video, the scene bounces from the dash of the pickup to quick views of the fence. You can't hear the narration over the engine noise.)

"We are stopping at the barn," I say into the camera as I pan over the corrals to the gate. I want to get the gates in, the latches in particular.

"Let's go," says Mom. I lay the camera down and pull on my gloves. Then she hollers, "Grab your camera! Dad says we have to pull a calf!"

I jumped out of the pickup with camera in hand, racing through the gate to the pen inside the barn. What a film this was going to be!

There, staring at my mom and the dude-turned-photographer, is the mother cow. I say "mother" because beside her on the straw-covered floor of the pen is a newly born calf. Mom and I looked at each other. She hollered at Dad, "I thought you said we had to pull a calf?"

He hollered back, "I said, 'We got a good bull calf!' "

"Oh," we said.

Maybe he is right. They couldn't afford to have me, or others like me, up there all the time. But hey, I got another idea. Why not write a script about ranch life for a television sitcom?

I'd better call him. He'll love this idea!

# CHAPTER 3

# Seasons of Ranching

The tradition of neighbors helping one another with branding was born out of the need for more hands. The number of hired cowboys has diminished as have the bunkhouses that used to shelter them. Now cattle ranchers count on their neighbors.

"Thursday sounds good to me," Bud said to Sonny. "I'll be there."

Bud drove from his place on the Shields River. The seventy-two-year-old rancher crossed the Yellowstone River three times and drove around Livingston before he entered the Paradise Valley. The narrow lane down to his brother Sonny's place was tree-lined and steep. "Sure a good set of buildings," he mused. "Don't see many of those old peak-roofed barns still standing."

Bud was surprised. It was a few minutes before 3 p.m. and there were no other outfits in the yard yet.

"I don't have any wrestlers," Sonny answered when asked. "Couldn't find any young fellers around." He poured more water in the coffeepot. A visitor was never sure how old a "fresh" pot of coffee was at the seventy-eight-year-old bachelor's house.

"Pour me a cup and give me a knife to cut it," joshed Bud as he grabbed the well-worn phone book and started calling. "Looks like rain—maybe brandin's a no-go anyhow." He had made six calls in vain when a car drove up. In it were the cooks, Bud and Sonny's sisters,

Helen and Lillian. "You can always depend on family," said Bud as he greeted the pair. "No one would guess you two are over eighty!"

They didn't let that remark stand. After several minutes of teasing back and forth, Bud and Sonny brought in the boxes of groceries, pans and other items the two had deemed necessary for the branding dinner.

Bud was trying a few more calls when Hup Davis showed up, wearing his usual old battered black hat and black shirt. Hup could have played in any Western movie without changing the way he talked or dressed. His driver's license said he was seventy-eight years old, but he still looked as good on a horse as he had during the 1940s in his rodeo days.

"Yuh git anuther roper?" he asked as he looked suspiciously at the dark black coffee being poured into the thick old gray cup that used to be white.

"Buck . . . Buck Chaney's s'posed ta come." Sonny poured some more water in the coffeepot. Lillian and Helen were scrubbing on the stove and washing up the dishes piled in the sink.

"How's old Buck doing?"

"Well, he was glad to see his seventy-seventh birthday this spring. Without that heart bypass, he'd be six feet under. Looks like his rig at the barn just now," Sonny said as he glanced out the window.

"Looks like I'm the only able body here," joked Gary Cotant as he hung his oil-stained hat on a peg by the door. He was followed by Larry McComb.

Larry sank down in a chair. "Pour me some of that black lead, Sonny." Larry was undergoing chemo for the cancer he had been battling the last two years. "Don't be proud, Gary . . . we are both close to bein' senior citizens."

Bud was quietly sitting in an old wooden chair over by the phone. He knew they still needed some able-bodied wrestlers for those big calves. "How many you got corralled up?" He asked his brother.

"Right 'round a hundred, give or take."

"Valerie's coming to help," said Helen. No one hollered, "Terrific!" How could an Arizona State University art graduate visiting her grandparents be of any help? She could paint like a professional, but wrestle a 125-pound calf? One that had to be held still while a red-hot iron sizzled a mark of ownership to this ranch?

It was 5 p.m. and drizzling rain when they headed toward the round corral. The youngest of the Bohleen brothers, Andy, arrived with his son, Dan. "Cal and Suzie were right behind us as we crossed the river," said Andy. One boot was worn more than the other. He had lost some toes to an oil drill in Wyoming in the '50s. He spoke a few understanding words to McComb as they lit the propane torch for the branding irons. Andy had gone through radiation and chemo a few years back himself.

They all went over to help Suzie get Calvin out of the specially equipped van. Since his dad, the eldest Bohleen brother, had died a few years ago after a horse fell with him, they all considered Cal "their kid." They were mighty proud of Cal and Suzie too.

Calvin was injured during a bull ride in a rodeo in 1968. He was paralyzed from the shoulders down and has been a wheelchair since then. He and Suzie have made a very successful life with their cattle-buying business, ranching and his art. Since rodeo has always been in the Bohleen blood, the camaraderie disallows pity. Faith in God permeates this family, a heritage passed down through generations. Some are more open and bold in their walk with God, others quietly trusting God to "work all things together for good for those who love Him" (see Romans 8:28).

"Well, whatcha waitin' for . . . the moon to rise?" Cal's motorized wheelchair bumped and swayed as he blew in a narrow tube by his shoulder to direct his chair to the fence. "Suz is ready, she's a pro at vaccinating! She practices on me all the time!" he hollered.

Larry leaned off his horse and threw the gate open so the other two ropers, Hup and Gary, could ride through. Andy arranged the irons on the old oil barrel that had been cut with a welding torch to hold the irons and keep them in the red-hot fire inside. Then he turned the propane up a notch. If those irons weren't hot enough, he'd hear about it. *No matter how old you get, you are still the "young one"!* he thought to himself with a smile.

Bud was sitting in the dirt showing Valerie the way to hold a bawlin', kickin' calf, when one of the phone calls bore fruit. Three teenage ranch kids from up the valley hauled themselves over the fence. "Wrestlers, heads up," yelled Hup as he dragged in the first calf. From there the process was as synchronized as an Olympic swimming drill. The ropers didn't miss a loop. They'd done this for decades. The calves were cut, vaccinated and branded. Good-natured razzing was drowned out by the bellowing, concerned mother cows crowded outside the corral. One by one, the hundred (give or take) calves got the X REVERSE F BRAND.

"Yuh done good!" was a huge compliment given more than once to Valerie as the crew washed up for supper. Chairs scraped the new linoleum just put down on the old ranch house kitchen floor a few weeks ago as food was placed on the oilcloth-covered table. They all bowed their heads as Bud offered a blessing in thanks for the Lord's strength and the soon-to-be devoured banquet meal.

Stories unfolded of past experiences in their younger days as they devoured the huge bowls of spuds and gravy. The plate overflowing with slices of roast beef was filled again and again by Helen and Lillian. "No more for me . . . oh, well, one piece of that pie," was the understated compliment for the cooks.

The dishes were washed and put away. A pot of "real" fresh coffee was made in a pot that had just one of its semiannual scrubbings. (The other comes at Thanksgiving when the entire clan gathers at Sonny's for the traditional dinner.) Story after story of experiences was told and laughter filled the house.

The moon was high in the sky when the gray coffee cups were shining white again and the dish towel was hung over the drainer.

Soon the slamming of horse trailer doors was followed by the sound of the engines of pickups and one van straining up the steep hill.

The calves were again snuggled securely close to their mothers in the pasture down by the river.

Not one of the participants thought the evening was out of the ordinary. It is a way of life. It has been for many years.

Alone once again, Sonny turned on his television for the news and sank into the old leather recliner next to the rolltop desk in the living room. He reached for his journal.

> Branded today. 103 calves, 67 heifers. Had enuff help. Helen and Lil cooked a good supper. Rained some.

Most couples celebrate fifty years of marriage with a party—guests, a big cake and lots of relatives.

"No way," my folks had said as we discussed the approaching event. "We don't want any fal-de-rah!" We talked about lots of options and finally the celebration for their golden anniversary was settled.

We just got back from the party. It was a week long.

We took them to the Calgary Stampede and the Edmonton Mall. It was their choice, and what fun we had! There were four generations of us on the trip. I had a huge lump in my throat and tears in my eyes as the grand entry paraded into the arena in front of us. The Canadian national anthem was played.

My folks had always wanted to see the Granddaddy of all Rodeos, and here we were. As the chuck wagons with drivers and riders raced in blazing colors at a terrifying speed around the track in front of us, Dad leaned over and said, "I sure did always want to see these races!" More tears ran down my face.

We toured the zoo and a tractor junk yard, and we women got a black belt in shopping at the mall. We had fun! But fifty years of marriage or not, there is work to be done—hay to be baled and stacked, you know. As we turned south, I heard Dad telling Mom, "We better stop and pick up a bale or two of twine when we get to Great Falls."

What a party! Happy fiftieth, Mom and Dad.

By the way, did I miss the cake?

My mom had to have most of the little finger on her right hand amputated two weeks ago. She and Dad had been getting ready to brand a few late calves. She had a lariat in her hand, and when she went to catch her horse she decided just to loop the rope around her horse's neck instead of going to the barn for a halter. When she opened the gate, another horse bolted through beside her. This scared her horse, and before she could blink, the rope wrapped around her hand with the full weight of the horse behind it. If she hadn't been wearing gloves, she would have lost all her fingers.

"Why didn't you let Dad drive you to the hospital?" I asked when she called. "You might have fainted on the way!"

"Because I thought he might have fainted!" she retorted. My dad rose to his own defense when I went to visit her in the hospital after the surgery. He said he saw her coming across the field leading her horse with "way too much slack." He took a look at her bloody glove and said she probably should go to the doctor and get it looked at. Neither of them knew how bad it really was. He would meet her at the house after he closed the gates and put the horses in the corral. When he got to the house she was already gone.

"So I figured she'd be back in an hour or a little longer if she needed some stitches. I went ahead and saddled the horses and got the stuff ready for branding." It wasn't too long before Dad got a call to come to town. She was in surgery. They said they were trying to save her fingers. He took off in a flash and the twelve miles to town were spent praying while he drove.

A week of agonizing pain later, they decided her little finger could not be saved. The other fingers would be OK. When I called last week, she had mowed the lawn and hauled some hay bales. "That is why I am a city wife," I told her.

This week I just want to tip my cowboy hat (which sits idly on my closet shelf most the time) to ranch women. This same week, Margaret Porter, a Rosebud County lady rancher, lost one of her fingers while she was pulling a calf.

You ranch women are a hardy lot. You can don a beautiful garment and gather appreciative compliments. You can be eloquent and loving. You can prepare banquets on a moment's notice and keep a home attractive and comfortable. You rear children and meet their needs while mothering calves, lambs, colts and baby chicks. You can prepare a dinner for twenty men for branding and run to town in the middle of the morning to get forgotten ear tags. You go to town shopping and add tractor parts, a trip to the bank and the vet, and still call home to see if there is anything else you should pick up! Many of you can change a tire, rope a calf, make a shirt and cook circles around Betty Crocker.

You are a ranch lady. You are an inspiration. I salute you!

The calendar on the ranch doesn't read by months or weeks; it is winter feeding, calving, branding, farming, irrigating, haying, shipping and then Thanksgiving and Christmas. Each one of these divisions of time is measured by when the job gets done, with weather being the variable most of the time. When the freshly baled hay is all stacked and the farm equipment parked until next year, it is time for the fall roundup of the cattle from summer pasture and the sale of this year's calf crop. On most ranches, steers (boy calves) are sold to feed lots with some of the heifers (girl calves) kept for replacement stock.

My folks shipped their calves on Saturday. Translated for the city-bred, that means the independent businessman brought his product to market. For the rancher, it is the day of reckoning.

Invested in the product (calves) are feed costs, health care, pasture, labor, taxes and general ranch maintenance. There is interest on the loan at the local bank to buy the aforementioned. Then the investment of the rancher's time and labor to keep those calves alive from birth to market. The labor is directly proportional to the hardness of the winter and the spring moisture. Most folks go to a job knowing the amount of money they will earn. For the stock grower, there is always an element of risk. It depends on market price and the weight of the calves.

When October approaches, the stress starts up the spine of the individual stock owner. He has read market reports and listened to the agricultural news on the local radio station. He has an idea of the price of livestock around the nation. But the final sale comes down to the offer. The prospective buyer offers a price per pound for the calves. Then the fall guessing game starts. Is the market going higher or lower?

The rancher thinks back. Four years ago he sold at 64 cents and two weeks later the price was 69 cents. Year before last, he toughed it out waiting for a better offer. He lost a dime per pound. If he sells at 74 cents and the neighbor down the creek gets 79 two weeks later, he won't sleep for weeks. If he doesn't take the 74-cent offer and the market drops every day thereafter, he will kick himself the rest of the winter—of course, he won't sleep then, either.

He takes an offer and sets a shipping date. The year's earnings will be determined by the weight of the calves. The rattle of the scales will tally his income.

Stock trucks line up at the shipping yards. Surprisingly, there is not a lot of tension on the weather-beaten faces. This is not new to them. This is a way of life. They've been here before. This year's stock prices are up. But so are the expenses.

"You win some, you lose some," says Hank as he walks back to his truck. "Sure thought they'd weigh more."

Grandpa, Hank's dad, walking slower with a cane to strengthen worn-out legs, says, "Well, that bottomland just needed more moisture. But it could have been worse. Back in '85 . . . " The rest of his sentence is lost as he labors up into the truck.

In an old International stock truck, a husband and wife lean back against the seat. "We did it. Another year is ours." They sit rejoicing that the bank will not be able to foreclose on them this year. The payment will be made.

Across the way, another rancher jumps into his truck. It too has seen better days. He takes off his hat and bows his head. "Thank You for meetin' our needs. You have never failed us yet. I just wanted to say thanks, Lord. Those calves of Yourn and mine weighed in right respectable."

The trucks pull out of the shipping yards. The ranchers will all be meeting down at the Trail Rite Inn, a local café—a twenty-year tradition of saluting the departing stock. No one asks the weight of his neighbor's calves or the price he got. That information always comes secondhand. "I heard the Double U got 73 cents" or "Joe said the Curtis calves averaged 520." Asking weights and prices is in as bad taste as asking a man how much he makes or how much money he has in the bank.

In this business, the talk centers around the "ifs." If it rains. If the hay price is up. If the interest rate is down. If it snows. If the calving goes smoothly. There are no slumped shoulders around the table as the coffee cups are refilled. There are no newcomers to reckoning day here. When the grain is harvested, the hay stacked, the alfalfa seed cleaned or the pigs loaded, the game of risk is run again. The profit will be in the tip of the scales and the going market price.

Their camaraderie has given them a good time. But the chores are waiting. They grab their hats and tease the waitress as they pay their tab. Beside the cash register is a plastic box with a roll of bright, foil-covered Montana lottery tickets. No one buys a chance. The Big Spin doesn't excite these folks.

# CHAPTER 4

# The Dude Gets a Promotion

**T**hings are lookin' up!" I say to myself as I breeze through the field, the cold air whipping my face. I don't mind the cold. I don't know how it has happened, but it is the first morning at the ranch for calving season this year and—get this—I get a brown Carhartt coat and a four-wheeler to ride!!

So I zoom through the field following my mom, who is riding Dad's four-wheeler. Dad is behind us on the tractor. I open the gates like a veteran. Dad feeds the cows some hay. We check future moms and then the nursery fields with moms and calves.

This is after drinking a pot of coffee sitting by the woodstove, prayer time together and a breakfast of oatmeal. (My favorite. Mom knows that.) Dad made the toast. First Dad had to go up Paradise Valley to Mill Creek where he bought some more hay. Mom and I think they have enough. Dad doesn't.

Mom has a hair appointment at Clyde Park. No working ranch wife has time to mess with hair stuff so she keeps it cut short in an easy do. Then we go on to Livingston for a few errands before Dad gets back. We have coffee with some friends, mail letters at the post office and look around town for Aunt Doris, Mom's sister. We don't find her. We shop a little and then eat an early lunch at Taco John's. I order us taco salads, potato oles and nachos. (I am dieting?) We catch up on family news. Mom calls home on the cell phone. (This modern invention is a gift from their daughter, the dude, and her husband. Although they protested at first, now they consider it a Godsend in their busy lives.) Dad is back at the ranch from hauling hay and wondering what's for lunch.

"On your own," says my mom.

"You can sure tell Lois is here!" says my dad.

"Open a can of soup," says Mom. "We'll be back shortly."

When we drive into the yard, we are amazed at how much it has warmed up. "We should pull the Toyota into town since it's so nice. Something is wrong with the fuel pump and it won't run," she explains. Dad agrees. He has just checked the maternity ward. All was well. So, after a little discussion over who was going to pull whom (been there?), Mom says, "Well, I am not about to be pulled by you two. No one will watch the road and you'll both be talking and waving your arms . . . I'll pull!"

We go in, leave the pickup at Larry's Fix-It place and then stop at Hardy's for ice cream and coffee. (I pass on the ice cream. I'm dieting.) Then back to the ranch where Dad decides that if we get hay in all the feeders tonight and if the weather is good and if no heifers are calving, we will drive over by Dillon to look at a horse he might buy.

So out we go. While I am breezing along, as I said, on my mechanical horse in style in my new-old brown Carhartt coat, I am thinking about writing about this experience for my column when I get home. I am so pleased with my "promotion" and how well I am doing this year.

Mom goes to the barn to let the ladies in waiting down to the creek for water. I follow Dad up to feed the first-year heifers and their calves. He waves me on when I go to shut the gate. I know we'll be right back through it.

I drive through the herd looking for any sickly calves . . . but mostly thinking about my column and phrasing words together . . . when out of the corner of my eye I see cows coming through the open gate—cows from the Waiting Field! I fly over the frozen cowpies and down through a ditch with more fear than good sense. Dad spots them at the same time. About ten get through before I get to the gate.

"Do I have to give the brown Carhartt coat back?" I ask the boss when he joins me at the gate—which is now closed, I might add.

"Not yet," he says. He and Mom get on the four-wheeler with the dude on the back, quite subdued.

"It's just nice when it's someone else who left the gate open," he says over his shoulder to me (who's hanging on for dear life).

If you have had to run the gate while cutting cows, you know how much fun that is. If you have never had the pleasure, don't yearn for it. It is my least favorite job. Actually, I hate it. But with the score in the minus column of my time sheet today, I get off at the gate and stand ready.

I won't tell you the whole story, just this: while running to get out of the way and then spinning around to follow the cow so she won't turn back after she gets through the gate, my head gets going faster than my feet. At least I think that is what happens. I find myself flying through the air, landing with an "OOOMMPH!" right on my taco salad and potato oles! Mom and Dad head after another cow, so I just get up, manage to suck some oxygen into my lungs somehow and hunker back over to "my" gate.

Later, back at the barn, I tell them I had flown through the air and landed with a thud. After reassurances that I am all in one piece, they both start laughing. "You had quite a first day," Mom says.

Dad just looks at Mom and says, "Tonight you can write in your diary, 'Lois got in a footrace with a cow today. Lois took second.' "

So that is the first day. I think I have to go to bed now. My bones tell me it is time. (I put my new-old brown Carhartt coat under my bed . . . just in case anyone is looking to take it away from me. . . .)

On the second day, the need for much prayer is evident. "I think I need prayer for bravery," I say as we share prayer requests and coffee in the living room of my parents' log home. (I had said the same to Robert the night before when we had our nightly chat and prayed together over the phone. It's a habit we try not to miss even when we are apart. It took my cancer to get us started several years ago.)

This large living room is such a comfortable place. Western paintings and trophy elk and deer antlers share the walls with the black bear rug. Big picture windows on three sides of the living room let in the morning sun as it comes up, coating the snow on the ground with a silver glaze. A view of three ranges of mountains gives new meaning to "purple mountains majesty." An open Bible lies beside Dad's chair along with *Our Daily Bread*. He always gets up early—very early—and has his devotions first. Mom likes to read her Bible and read her women's devotional book before she goes to bed. I didn't read my Bible last night. I told God I would just quote some Bible verses as I fell asleep. I think I said two.

"Tear up to the green gate, open it and get out of the way."

"Hustle up to the barn and open the gate for the heifers."

"We got to git to gittin'—on the double!"

Those are the directives for the dude, heard over and over. No wonder my folks stay so young—age can't catch up with them. This morning we really have to hustle. Dad found one new calf at 4:30 a.m. when he got up to check the cows. He had carefully penciled "#91, heifer" and the date in the tally book by his chair when he came in.

There was another one—#78 had a bull calf—when we went out to check before breakfast. Both were doing fine; it was a nice day, 50 degrees above zero.

I open the gate.

"Open the gate this way," Mom hollers, motioning in, as she rides up on her four-wheeler behind me. We have to run #91 mom-cow and her calf across the creek to the nursery field. Number 91 needs to stay in the corral to make sure the calf is sucking.

"Yesterday you said I should always open it the other way," says the dude, now an authority on gates.

"That's right. Unless we are running a cow through, and then you open it the other way."

"No wonder I can never get it right—the rules keep changing," I retort as I jump on my four-wheeler to get out of the way. No matter where I park the dumb thing, it is always in the way.

We feed and then change clothes to go to Sheridan, further west in Montana, near Dillon, to look at a horse Dad is interested in. "The weather is good so we better go while we can," he had said this morning. It is at least a two-hour drive.

By the time we get to Twin Bridges, we are in a real blizzard. Three calls on the cell phone finally get us to the right place. "We better hustle," Dad says as we get out of the car. "We could be getting calves in this weather." We walk to the barn and meet the ranch lady and Jake, the horse. We all like him. Dad says he'll take him. They make arrangements and we walk back up the lane to the car.

"It's sure a good thing we weren't over here to look at a refrigerator," my mom quips. We all laugh, knowing that if we had been shopping for an appliance instead of for a horse, the roads would have been *far* too bad for Dad to set out at all. . . .

We stop at Three Forks at Wheat Montana where they harvest and sell their products right on their farm. Mom buys some wheat. I do too.

"I'll put it in the root cellar with my twenty pounds of rice," I say. "You know I told Robert I got it in case there was a disaster. He told me if he had to eat all that rice, he hoped he'd perish in the disaster!"

Back home and back into cow clothes.

We have a calf and it is cold. "We got to get it under the heat lamp right away!" Dad says. Again there is some discussion over who was going to lift what, yet we manage to get the calf on the back of Mom's four-wheeler.

"You'll have to hold it on," he tells me. Mom gets on the four-wheeler facing north. I get on with her, facing south. (You get the picture?) I am holding on for dear life to the wiggling, too-froze-to-bawl calf. The mom-cow has her nose next to mine. I see myself as a rodeo clown with no barrel to hide in. Down the hill, across the creek, up the hill and through the gate, down the road to the barn and through the gate, I hang on to the little black calf. The mom-cow is never more than seven inches from my face the whole way. I figure the baby calf was the only one more scared than I was.

Dad is already at the barn and has the gates open. By the time we get the new baby under the heat lamp in calf ICU and the mom-cow in the pen with fresh straw and the feeding done, the storm is over. We go to the house. Daylight is gone. We change clothes again to go to town for Bible study. When we get back home, we change clothes again. Dad and I go up to check for calves. There aren't any. The last clothes change of the day is into my pajamas.

"Wake me up when you have to go up," I tell him. "I'll go with you."

Yeah, right. I fall asleep the minute my head hits the pillow. I don't hear him get up at 4 or again at 6. I am sawing logs while standing in front of a rodeo chute in my clown outfit. This ranch stuff is tough on a dude.

Day Three. After a pot of coffee around the woodstove (we sit close this morning—it's -20 outside!) and our precious prayer time, we have a breakfast of oatmeal and toast.

Like most kids, "give 'em an inch and they'll take a mile," right? Two days on the four-wheeler and now I think I am a pro. I have learned to shift Dad's four-wheeler without grinding the gears. I can start it without help. I am good.

When Dad signals from the cab of the tractor that he is going from the hay corral to the field with the heifers in it, I know the routine. I have to open the green gate ahead. Since I just got back on my mechanical horse after closing the hay corral gate, I say to myself, "Lois, just zip past the tractor and get the gate open before he gets there." I pull alongside the tractor, loaded with a bale in front and one in back—and realize I am scared. The road tilts on both sides. I am a chicken when it comes to side hills. (When mowing at our place north of Colstrip, I always switch from the tractor lawn mower to the push one when I'm mowing the hillside along our pond. I just get scared.) Scared I am, as I try to pass Dad and the tractor. From cocky to scared in one instant. In panic, I just turn left without looking.

Only left is straight down the hill at that particular place! In my terror, I totally forget about having a brake. It never enters my mind. I am speeding straight down the hill screaming "YIKES!" at the top of my lungs.

That terror is replaced by panic-praying as I see a four-foot dropoff where the water has run down the hill. I know I am going over that drop to my doom. Just then, I have a moment of clear thinking. (God does answer kids' prayers!)

When we used to snowmobile with friends, they got tired of having to stop and dig Lois out of whatever snowbank she got stuck in, time after time. The men told me, "Lois, if you think you are in trouble, gun it—and you won't get stuck!" Obediently, I did that and it always worked. I know I am in trouble as I head for the dropoff with no where else to go, so I gun it. And fly to the other side of the gully, landing upright and on all fours!

Mom is right there when I get stopped. "You can go home right now," she says. "Your dad and I can't handle anymore scares like that!"

Dad says, "That four-wheeler came up a foot in the back when you went over that bank!" I know they are both thanking God that I am OK.

As with most lessons we got as "kids," they don't have to say much. I get the message. The lesson is learned. I become quite a docile rider on my mechanical horse after that. They let me stay. After all, it is only 10 a.m. on Day Three. Maybe they could make a hand out of me yet.

We have to catch Digger, Dad's horse he is replacing with Jake, so he can be sold—and somebody needs to open the gates!

The morning after my near-wreck on the four-wheeler, our prayer time is permeated with thanksgiving for God's protection. "You better keep your wits about you, Lois, or you'll get your four-wheeler and your brown Carhartt taken away," they kid me.

Our first job on this day is to catch the horse. The horses are in winter pasture on the east end of the ranch. The new horse, Jake, will be delivered in a couple of weeks. Dad already has a buyer for Digger. A blood test, called a Coggins Test, has to be made on any horse being transported in Montana. The vet is coming at 11 o'clock to do the blood test. It takes seven to ten days for results. If we take the vial of blood over to the lab at Montana State University in Bozeman, thirty-eight miles away, we can get the results the next day. So that is our plan.

But first we have to tube a calf whose mom-cow wasn't letting it suck. We have to run them into the barn. The mom-cow is on the fight. I try to be brave. After all, I have on brown clothes. The mom-cow lowers her head and paws the dirt in front of me.

"Shut the gate!" my dad yells. I am in reverse already. Me the rodeo clown. I am in a dead heat with the angry cow for the gate, but I get there first.

"Good job!" Dad says as we get back to the house. I feel vindicated.

I park my "horse" in the driveway and race into the house to change to town clothes to go to Bozeman. Mom puts the vial of blood she got from the vet, wrapped in plastic, into an empty coffee can. We change clothes and go out to the garage to get in the car. As usual, my four-wheeler is parked in the wrong place—behind the car.

"I'll move it," I tell my dad. I set the coffee can with the blood sample on a chair in the garage.

"No, I'll get it, you got your clean clothes on." So I get in the car. Mom takes the driver's seat and backs out of the garage. We are on our way for our quick trip. Robert has relayed several messages for speaking engagements to me that morning, so I use the cell phone to contact various people while Mom drives. It is the first spare moment I have had all morning. We get to the overpass where Highway 89 meets with I-90 when I finish my calls. "That's done," I say to Mom.

"Just checking—we've got the blood sample, haven't we?" Mom asks.

"Yup," I say, "right . . . " I search the car. No coffee can. No blood sample. Sheepishly, I dial the ranch. Dad answers right away. "Ummmmmm, could you look in the garage and see if the blood sample is there?"

Sure enough, it is right on the chair where I left it. Mom makes a U-turn and back we go to the ranch. Dad meets us in the yard, coffee can in hand. "You don't have to say a thing," I say.

"It's a good thing we didn't get to Bozeman before we found it missing," says my mom, ever the optimistic one.

Maybe that's why they still always call me the "kid." At least they can still hope I will grow up, mature and amount to something!

"If it isn't water, water, water," said the mother of the dude, "it's hay, hay, hay!"

"You forgot 'too much rain, not enough rain.'" We were bouncing along in the little blue pickup, now running smoothly, to do some fencing.

"I don't have a chance with you two," retorted Dad, laughing as he said it.

"It's just because we both know you so well," I said. And in the middle of the teasing, I was filled with a sudden rush of emotions. How many "kids" can spend time like this with their folks? How many husbands are so supportive of their wives' folks and encourage helping out in any way? I know I am blessed. Just watching my parents inspires me. The partnership in their marriage for nearly sixty years would be a good model for the rest of us.

"Stop right here," said Dad. "We'll unroll this wire first." We hopped out of the pickup. The plan for the day was to put up electric fence. Then we would move the cows that had calved into the sixty (not only do we number cows out west, but some of us number fields too). The bulls were in the pasture by the creek. They would need electric shock therapy to keep their romantic tendencies in check. (Dad didn't say that. He wouldn't. That is dude-interpretation.) When their noses or shoulders touch the fence, that little buzz changes their minds about pushing through the fence.

"Did I tell you about Tyler and the ear tags?" I asked. They said I hadn't. These grandchildren, their great-grandchildren, are precious to them, and they love having an active part in their lives. Tyler was four at the time.

"We were driving out on Sarpy Creek Road so I could find some flat rocks for our steps. We took Justin and Tyler with us. We had just come over a hill and Robert was driving through open range with cows on both sides of the road. Tyler looked them all over, then looked at Grampi and said, 'Why do all those cows have price tags in their ears?' Robert almost drove off the road laughing." Mom and Dad laughed too.

We unrolled the roll of wire along the fence line a half mile. Then we had to go down a hill, across the creek and up the bank on the other side. We drove around to the other side of the creek and unloaded the battery that would power the fence.

"Don't you even smile," I told my dad. "I am older and smarter now. I am not going to test the fence!" I knew he was thinking back to those childhood days of mine on the ranch. It was a lot like some people who get toddlers to taste a lemon or a pickle—just to see the expression on their faces. Dad was always trying to get my brother, Ron, or me to "test" the fence to see if it was on. Naturally, the "bite" would send him into gales of laughter.

One of the tales that gets told over and over is when I, at the wise age of ten, said, "No, I'm not going to do it, I won't touch it with my fingers. Give me the pliers, I'll test it with them!"

"I wasn't even thinking that," Dad said with a smile.

"Yeah, sure," I said. We hooked up the battery. Mom handed him the yellow wire to hook to the fence.

"Y-OUCH!"

Mom and I fell on the creek bank in gales of laughter. After rubbing his hand a bit, Dad laughed too. Finally—we got him! It may be shocking (!) for you to believe that a nice Christian family could act like this. But that's the way it is. I always tell people that when I grew up, we worked together and we played together. We cried together and we laughed together.

Maybe that is why my emotions run so deep when I get the privilege of "helping" them now. I know that it doesn't just come easy to raise your kids. They would tell you they made mistakes back then. They would tell you that "by the grace of God" they raised my brother and me. I can tell you that it was love. We knew we were loved, no matter what we did. And the working and playing together, the crying and laughing together was a result of that. The fact that our parents lived their faith in God daily before our eyes gave Ron and me the example we needed to place our own faith in Jesus Christ.

As we started putting the staples in the fence posts, holding the wire in place, I held the wire and Dad nailed the staples. Mom had shut the battery off. I know because I asked her four times to make sure. We worked our way down the creek bank. I went first. I had my yellow boots on. I stepped into the creek. I sank into the mud and the water went right over the top of my boots. I heard laughter.

"You know," I said, "things haven't changed a bit on this place in fifty-eight years!"

But in my mind, I was making a mental note about a column I wanted to write about this day. I would call it a "Lesson from Fencing." It follows:

The dude was helping with the fencing. We were stringing up a wire to be powered with an electric charge from a battery to keep the cows in and the bulls out. We had strung the wire a half mile. The father of the dude pounded the staples into the posts to hold the wire in place. We walked back up the creek. "OK, turn it on!" hollered my dad to Mom. She was on the other side of the creek where a battery sat beside the fence line.

"You can be assured I am not going to touch it," I told him. Past experiences had taught me a lesson I hadn't forgotten.

"How could you think I would do such a thing?" said my dad with a smile. "We have a tester." He put one end of the tester in the dirt and touched the wire. A small lightbulb in the tester lit up. We were at the corner of the fence up the creek bank. But when we did the same thing on the next section of the fence, we had no charge, no light. "We've got a short somewhere. It has a ground somewhere." He explained that it had to be touching the barbed-wire fence along the line. We walked the line of fence twice. We couldn't find anything. We had a charge to the corner, then nothing. We walked the fence again, checking for branches, weeds or anything that could be causing the ground.

"Turn it on," we'd yell to Mom across the creek. Then, "Shut it off." We were checking it post by post.

"Hey, just a minute," said Dad. The wire we had strung was exactly parallel to the barbed-wire fence on the other side of the post. "You don't suppose the staple on this post is touching the staple that's holding the barbed wire up on the other side, do you?" he asked, not really asking me, but himself.

He pulled out the staple he had hammered in our new wire and hollered, "Turn it on!"

Sure enough, now the little lightbulb lit right up. "Can you believe that?" I said.

"Amazing!" he said. He hammered the staple back in at a different angle and then we picked up our stuff and headed back to the pickup. I couldn't help but think of a spiritual lesson.

Sometimes our relationship with God gets shorted out. Our prayers seem to hit the ceiling. We can't figure it out. Then we read a verse in the Bible or hear a sermon and it brings to mind a sin in our life. We confess it, ask God to forgive us and yes, the light comes back on. It isn't that we have lost our salvation or that God gives up on us. It's just that He wants us to be pure and holy before Him. That is why He gave us instructions in First John 1:9, "If we confess our sins, he is faithful and just to forgive us our sins, and to cleanse us from all unrighteousness" (KJV).

As we got out of the pickup in front of the house, I glanced at my four-wheeler. It had been quite a week. I hung my brown Carhartt coat up on a peg. It was time to pack up my suitcases and head back home. I had two months of speaking engagements on my schedule in front of me. It would be hard to leave. But I smiled as I put my suitcase in the car.

"God, You are so good. I know I am blessed. I have lots of lessons to share with the folks I'll be speaking to. That's the joy of walking with You. You teach us in everyday ways today, just as You did 2,000 years ago." My mind went to that verse in the gospel of John, "For God so loved the world, that he gave his only begotten Son, that whosoever believeth in him should not perish, but have everlasting life" (3:16, KJV).

Unconditional love. My parents are a product of that love. So am I. What a legacy for us to pass on to our children. God loves us even when He knows we sometimes fall short. "I get it, Lord," I said, as I put my turn signal on to swing onto I-90 to drive back to Colstrip after leaving the ranch. The four-wheeler, the brown Carhartt coat, opening the gates, fixing the fence, prayer time before we went to work each day, the oatmeal and the Bible studies—expression of love.

From the dude to the parents:

Thank you, I love you,
Lois

From the dude to her Lord:

Thank You. I love You,
Lois

# CHAPTER 5

# I'm Not Athletic and I Can't Cook

In spite of the fact that I can't cook, I'm not athletic, I have never won a beauty contest and my mind seems to be shrinking, there is one thing I know: God loves me anyway.

I learned about God when I was young. You know I was raised on a ranch in Montana. I have one brother. We worked together and we played together. We were a close family with lots of relatives nearby. On some weekends, we'd load the horses into a trailer and head for a rodeo. My dad rode bulls. Later my brother became a champion calf roper. Later I did some barrel racing. I was not a champion.

When I was about ten years old, my mom and dad went to hear a speaker at a church in town. They came home to tell us they had been "saved." I didn't know exactly what that meant, but our lives changed. I saw my mom become concerned about friends and relatives, telling them about Jesus. Jesus was her friend. God gave her a compassion for others and a willingness to help anyone anytime. She was always ready to help out at our church, the Livingston Bible Church, whenever they needed any help, even though she was busy at home as well. I can remember her often saying a prayer, "Lord, just help us get the work done!"

My dad changed too. He often had trouble with a temper. I saw that change as he fell humbly before the Lord. There was failure after failure at first. Then victory. He is such a loving, gentle, humble man today. Back then, I don't remember a night growing up that I didn't see him on his knees by the footstool in the living room, praying before he went to bed.

In the morning when I would get up, even with lots of chores to be done, there would be my mom and dad, reading the Bible and having devotions. Our weekends changed too. Now we would go to church first. Then we would load the horse trailer and head out for the rodeos. We went to church a lot. I memorized many Bible verses and Sunday school songs; I was always trying to be good! Many times I made trips to the altar pledging to be better. Those trips to the altar usually had something to do with sin and my brother.

We had a ditch that ran between the house and the barn. I would go out and jump across that ditch. Being tall and thin and two years older, I could easily jump to the bank on the other side. Then I'd say, "Come on, Ronnie, you can do it!" With lots of encouragement, he'd try . . . and fall in. He would go crying to the house. (You know how little brothers are!)

This was in the days before automatic washers and six pairs of jeans. My mom would hang the little Levis on the line and tell him, "If you fall in one more time, you will get a licking!" (They had those in the olden days too.)

I couldn't wait to get back out to that ditch. I'd jump across and say, "Come on, Ronnie, you can do it. You only missed it by two inches last time!"

Of course he'd fall in and get in trouble and I would be glad, until I sat in church the next Sunday! Then I would feel terrible and promise God to be good—again.

It was a grand life, growing up in a family filled with love and good times. When I was fifteen, I told everyone I was going to Africa to be a missionary. When I was sixteen, I told everyone I was going to New

York to be a model. When I was eighteen, I enrolled at Montana State College at Bozeman to study home economics. Now don't laugh. I can't cook, but I can sew. If you want me to sew you up an outfit, I can do it. You'll just have to provide the meals while I sew.

There wasn't going to be any of this ranch life, prairie stuff for me. I was going off for a career and to find the man of my dreams. He didn't come riding up on a horse either.

My folks gave me the car for a Sunday afternoon. I was a senior in high school. I picked up a girlfriend. We went cruisin'—which in Livingston was one city block that we drove around and around and around . . . that is where the gas shortage came from a decade later. As we were driving around we saw these two guys in a car with MSC college stickers in the back window. I said, "Those are college guys! Let's get them to notice us!" (which clearly shows my priorities in those days).

They didn't seem to notice us. So I drove down a one-way alley the wrong way, and we both leaned out the window and yelled—and they noticed us!

We said, "We will meet you at the morgue."

Don't laugh. That is where the kids all met. If there wasn't a funeral, there was always lots of parking!

These two guys got out of their car and walked up to us. Leaning their elbows on the bottom of the open window, they peered into the car and said, "How'd cha like to get in and ride around with us?" (Where the inflection is in that statement depends on whether you are hearing this story from me or him.)

I said, "Oh, no you don't. My parents are very strict. One of their rules is that I cannot ride around with strangers in their cars. But HOW'D CHA LIKE TO GET IN AND RIDE AROUND WITH US?"

And that is how I met my husband.

We were married in September 1961 after my freshman year of college and his junior year. We learned about surviving on deer meat, beans and donations from relatives. After college, we moved to Great Falls where Robert got a job with Montana Power. I got a job as Cascade County Extension Agent (in sewing, not foods). We had one son born in Bozeman and three years later our second son was born in Great Falls.

I was still being good. We went to church on Sundays. I quoted all those Bible verses I had memorized in Sunday school years before. I told the people that my mom and dad were Christians, my grandparents were Christians and my Great-Aunt Ruth was one of the first Christian and Missionary Alliance missionaries in the Philippines. We were in. I was helping in the church nursery and was in charge of Vacation Bible School. Robert was transferred to Billings and our third son was born there. We had a nice house in a nice neighborhood.

And we were attending a nice church. It was a Christian and Missionary Alliance Church. It was close to our house. They were glad to hear about my Great-Aunt Ruth. As soon as we arrived I told them "my folks were Christians, my grandparents . . . my Great-Aunt Ruth . . ." That year I was in charge of Vacation Bible School at that church.

Within two weeks of moving to Billings and finding a church home, I was visited by two ladies from that church. One of the ladies invited me to attend a Christian Women's Club meeting and give a special feature on sewing.

I had never heard of the group. They said it was held at the Lake Hills Country Club. I thought it was probably a nice place for a nice person like me to go to. So I said, "Yes." The luncheon was nice, the people were nice, the decorations were nice and I thought the special feature was excellent! So when it came time to fill out their little yellow guest slip, I noticed a box at the bottom where it said, "Check if you would like to help in any way you can." I checked the box. The next month I was the new decorations chairman of Billings Christian Women's Club (CWC). Nice, huh?

A perfect life. I still couldn't cook. I wasn't athletic. But I went to church and I was very nice.

Have you got me psychoanalyzed? The things that were really important to me were looking good and being good. However, at this time in my life, this nice church lady got to doing some serious thinking. And watching and listening. I started watching the women at CWC, the speakers, the other gals on the committee and the women in my church. Lots of them were not shallow. Looking good was not at the top of their lists of priorities. I started listening to Christian radio and the speakers on it. I started listening, really listening, to the sermons at my church. I started thinking about some of those Bible verses that I had memorized years before. And I started reading and studying my Bible—for me.

I saw myself still as that twelve-year-old girl, trying to be good enough for God. Only now it wasn't my brother that was tripping me up, it was just life.

No, it wasn't just life—it was just me. Trying to be good enough for God. I was building a little house on my prairie, all right. But I was doing it myself, brick by brick: a brick of daily Vacation Bible School, a brick of nursery duty, a brick of CWC, even a brick of baked beans to the potluck suppers now and then.

I memorized a verse years ago that said, "For no one can lay any foundation other than the one already laid, which is Jesus Christ" (1 Corinthians 3:11). I could stack all the bricks I wanted on my dirt for my little house, but those good-works bricks wouldn't do. God's Word said (and I had memorized this one too, from Ephesians 2:8-9, KJV), "For by grace are ye saved through faith; and that not of yourselves: it is the gift of God: not of works [i.e., VBS, CWC, church, etc.]." Right there I saw myself, trying to be good enough for God. The Bible also says, "All have sinned and fall short of the glory of God" (Romans 3:23). Even church ladies.

Then I came to a realization. God had a blueprint for me. A plan for all of us. We read it on our Christmas cards: "For unto you is born this day in the city of David a Saviour, which is Christ the Lord" (Luke 2:11, KJV).

I knelt beside my bed. I said through tears, "Forgive me for trying to do it my way. Jesus, come into my life. You be in charge. I will follow Your building plans from now on, believing that You are who You say You are and that Your Word, the Bible, is for me." From my former cowgirl days I said, "I am turning the reins over to You."

My life is different because of that day. He has changed and blessed the direction of my life. Oh, I still couldn't cook. I still wasn't athletic. But my foundation was different, because my foundation was built on Him. Yes, storms did come. Storms of three teenage boys (got any kids?) but blessings also. Storms of financial woes (had any kids in college?). Storms of job security, moving, relationships with friends, illness. Cancer? You might call that a storm!

But I am here to tell you—God never fails! In storms, He gives peace. In storms, He gives comfort and joy. In storms, He causes the clouds to part and the sun to shine through.

He has a plan. I trust Him. He is putting the bricks together on my house now and He is the Master Builder.

I can't cook.

I'm not athletic.

Sometimes I am not even very nice.

But God loves me—and He loves you too.

Who is building your house?

Read through these verses with me:

**Matthew 7:24-29**: Therefore whosoever heareth these sayings of mine, and doeth them, I will liken him unto a wise man, which built his house upon a rock: and the rain descended, and the floods came, and the winds blew, and beat upon that house; and it fell not: for it was founded upon a rock. And every one that heareth these sayings of mine, and doeth them not, shall be likened unto a foolish man, which built his house upon the sand: and the rain descended, and the floods came, and the winds blew, and beat upon that house; and it fell: and great was the fall of it. And it came to pass, when Jesus had ended these sayings, the people were astonished at his doctrine: For he taught them as one having authority. (KJV)

**Revelation 3:20**: Behold, I stand at the door [of your house], and knock: if any man [or woman or boy or girl] hear my voice, and open the door, I will come in to him, and will sup with him, and he with me. (KJV)

**Romans 10:8-13**: For salvation that comes from trusting Christ—which is what we preach—is already within easy reach of each of us; in fact, it is as near as our own hearts and mouths. For if you tell others with your own mouth that Jesus Christ is your Lord, and believe in your own heart that God has raised him from the dead, you will be saved. For it is by believing in his heart that a man becomes right with God; and with his mouth he tells others of his faith, confirming his salvation. For the Scriptures tell us that no one who believes in Christ will ever be disappointed. Jew and Gentile are the same in this respect: they all have the same Lord who generously gives his riches to all those who ask him for them. Anyone who calls upon the name of the Lord will be saved. (TLB)

You can pray right now, right where you are and invite Jesus into your life. You can even say it as I did: "God, I want You in my life. Forgive my sin. Come into my life. I'm handing the reins of my life over to You." Amen and AMEN!!!

# CHAPTER 6

# I'm Not Athletic and
I Can't Cook—Really!

Decmber 31: Reflecting. Evaluating. Praying. I list my goals and steps to victorious living.

1. *Devotions every morning before going to work.* Starting with Matthew will prevent getting bogged down in the Old Testament as in years past.
2. *Exercise and diet.* Continue CPRD (local health club) exercise, going every lunch hour for the next two weeks to make up for holidays. Cut out sweets.
3. *Writing will be the highest priority.* The end of my book in sight. Tenacity will be the key.
4. *Cooking.* (Contributes to good health!) Using computer recipe program and planning weekly menus are beginning steps.

I feel good. Resolve affirmed. I carry a plate of holiday goodies to the couch. A video and a box of chocolates round out my evening. (One last time.)

**January 1:** Sleep until 10 a.m. This is a holiday. Earl Murray's *Thunder of the Dawn* is on the nightstand. I am enthralled with the writing ability of this former Colstrip resident. It would be good for me to finish the book, a Christmas gift. (I'll be more inspired to write.) I get a plate of holiday goodies. Should get those all eaten up before I diet. Robert and I go out for a late lunch. No groceries for cooking yet. I will need to make a menu.

10:00 p.m. Guilt. Remorse. Resolve reaffirmed. After all, it was a holiday.

**January 2:** Early church, barely make it in time. Eat out. (We always eat out on Sundays after church.) Nap. Finish goodies and movies. It was so cold outside.

10:00 p.m. Guilt. Contrition. Resolve reaffirmed. After all, tomorrow is Monday.

**January 3:** Holiday from work. Sleep in. Must take advantage of day off. Call Todd and Lisa, "Can Justin come spend the day?" Need quality time with grandchild. At 7:00 p.m. take Justin home and pick up Lisa and Mary to go to Alliance Women meeting. No one comes. We have the wrong night. Go to Coal Bowl for sundaes since we're out.

10:00 p.m. Still have hope. After all, tomorrow . . .

**January 4:** Pray and read first two chapters of Matthew before work. Pack gym bag for CPRD at noon. Forgot Tuesday is my lunch date with Evelyn. Will go to CPRD tonight. Forgot, can't tonight. Must do checkbook and bills.

11:00 p.m. Tomorrow . . .

**January 5:** Pray and read chapter 3 of Matthew. Apple for breakfast. Pack gym bag. Drats! Forgot hair appointment after work. Must go to post office, mail bills and do banking at lunch. Tenant brings goodies to our office. OK to eat since I won't have time to eat at lunch. Call Robert, "Want to eat in town after my hair appointment? Then we can just go straight to prayer meeting at church." Write "MENU" on piece of scrap paper on my desk so I can start a grocery list.

7:00 p.m. Ask for prayer for "unspoken" prayer request. I need help!

**January 6:** Up late. Dash to work. Good thing gym bag is still in car. Boss reminds us we have awards luncheon at noon. Committee meeting in evening.

10:00 p.m. Despair. "Lois, you aren't good at anything! Spineless! No willpower. Now get a grip!"

**January 7, 8 and 9:** Start. Resolve reaffirmed. Blunder. Guilt. Try again . . . tomorrow.

This could really drive one nuts. But not me. A friend enlightened me. I am not a failure. I am an excellent starter. See—I'm writing!

"Did you have a good workout?" Robert asked

"Is that what you call it?" I snapped as I threw my gym bag on our bed. "I call it 'thirty minutes of being light-years out of my comfort zone!' " I hated PE in high school. I hated PE in college. I like donuts and hot fudge sundaes. I hate exercise. However, I also hate guilt. So I made up my mind to do this lunch hour exercise thing. (Probably the result of other people praying!)

After two weeks I have to admit it was OK. Don't get me wrong: it is not fun—just getting a little less uncomfortable. As a matter of fact, I just feel a mite good about doing something positive for my health. I feel so good I think I'll go get a donut! Just kidding. It is getting easier to go because I have found out the people are very nice. I forgive them all for (a) being skinny and (b) liking the place.

I still feel intimidated. My ability to enjoy moving my muscles was squelched years ago at Park County High School simply by passing the eighth grade. I went from a one-room country school with eighteen students to a high school in town with 400 students. Country school recess did not prepare me for PE classes.

At Grannis School, two miles on gravel road from my growing-up home in the country, all eighteen of us played sports together. In the winter we played "Fox and Geese" or ice skated on the creek that ran by the school yard. In the spring we captured frogs and made chains out of snake grass. Alice Martin and I tried playing jacks like the town kids did. There was no concrete in our school yard so we played jacks on the wooden porch, the only man-made flat surface. All we got was slivers.

We played "Annie-I-Over" the coal shed. We played "Roy Rogers and Dale Evans" when the girls won the vote. We played basketball, baseball, football and soccer when the boys won the vote. (Alice and I were always picked last.) Basically we had three daily recesses to be used in the activity of our (collectively, by vote) choice. We had lots of physical activity but no locker rooms.

When I went to high school in Livingston, I was introduced to PE classes, locker rooms and bare-naked showers with thirty strangers. Coming from a home where the word "pregnant" was not said out loud, the impact of this culture shock was forever a bad memory. Coupled with not having an athletic bone in my body, I vowed never to do this stuff if I became an adult—which at many times I thought I wouldn't, but would die on the gym floor. I coped by saying, "This too shall pass," which it did; although for some of the PE courses in college, the "passing" was barely.

Now here I am, many years later, submitting myself to the same old insecurities forming uncomfortable butterfly patterns in my belly. I said a prayer each day for my Lord to propel my feet into the exercise room.

As I was walking on the treadmill (Level 1, mountain 1) I mused, "Do you suppose most of the people who don't attend church feel about it as I do about this gym? Do you suppose somewhere in their past they 'got picked last' or had some experience that turned them off to church to this day?" I thought of my friend Phyllis. When I had first invited her to attend church with me, she routinely turned me down.

"What would I do there?" she said. "I haven't been inside a church in seventeen years. I'd feel so out-of-place. I don't even own a dress! And I wouldn't even know what door to go in. What if I ended up in the broom closet?"

Sounded just like me and CPRD, didn't it? Which made me wonder, while I was hanging on for dear life doing my treadmill thing, how many other situations where I feel perfectly at ease are uncomfortable and intimidating for others? What about social events, speaking before a group, working in an office, driving a car, taking a plane, relationships? Food (donuts come to mind) for thought, isn't it?

The way I see it, we have some choices: (a) just sit tight in the center of our personal comfort zone; or (b) grow some character by giving some old fears a run for their money.

Well, I've got my gym bag over my shoulder, my shower done (in this place they have doors!), and I just completed stepping out of my comfort zone for the twelfth time. Why don't you step out of yours and try (a) going to church or (b) tackling that other fearsome thing?

Employees of the company I worked for, the Montana Power Company, had to file a "Near-Miss Report" if they narrowly escaped an accident. I don't know if our local health club, CPRD, follows the same procedure, but just in case, here is my report:

**Time:** Lunch Hour
**Place:** Treadmill
**Persons Involved:** One—me
**Possible Accidents:**

1. Personal body getting slammed against the wall, crushing all life from my fragile being.
2. Getting sucked into mechanical jaws of inner belt loop by falling on belt while in motion. Entire body maliciously pureed, beginning with toes.
3. Having every shred of personal dignity stripped from body as tripping motion causes chin to catch on book rest on treadmill, nearly breaking nose as face swings by handrail while body continues to be propelled by the totally mindless, insensitive, black, serpentine, monster, grabbing, brainless treadmill.

**How Accident Was Averted:** Saved by God

My near-miss accident happened because I am getting so much more accomplished in my daily treadmill walking. Now I can go 3.2 miles per hour (Level 1) and think at the same time.

This week several of my friends and I needed the wisdom of God for some situations we were in. *I know what,* I said to myself. *You can pray while you tread!* The exercise room, which I call T.C. for Torture Chamber, was empty this noon. I set the digital screen for fifteen minutes at 3.3 miles per hour at Level 1. I decided to fold my hands in front of me on the book rest. That would help keep my balance (I'm still a little unsteady) and remind me that I was praying (because sometimes my mind wanders when I pray and I forget what I am doing).

Six minutes into my routine, my feet sent my brain an urgent message. The message from my feet to my brain was, *"We are going really really really fast!!"*

My eyes confirmed the message from my feet. The red digital speedometer was flashing "8.9 . . . 9.2 . . . 9.5 . . . 9.7 . . ."

I screamed, *"Whoa!"* (a holdover from my ranching background) and jumped to the side as I had seen other people do. This is the only thing that saved my body from being tossed through the air and slammed against the wall. The now vacant treadmill belt continued to race toward I don't know where.

As I caught my breath after my narrow escape, I saw the cause of my marathon dash. While resting my praying hands on the book rest, I had also unconsciously been pushing the + indicator on the digital speed control. Automatically the treadmill responded to what it assumed to be my request to increase speed! I said one more prayer before I headed to the shower, which was most definitely necessary on this day, "Thank You, Lord, for saving my life."

I had only one regret. I wish my personal trainer, Becky, had walked by while I was still in the Race Mode. I sure would have looked good!

My friends Peggy and Nancy went to Billings to meet Toni, who used to live in Colstrip, for the day. They decided to test-drive a sports car. It was hard to tell whether the salesperson or the three gals had the most fun when I listened to the hilarious report over coffee the next day.

Every three months, Kevin and Kelli make reservations for a room in a motel two hours from their home. They get a room with a hot tub. They spend the weekend flying kites and rekindling their marriage.

John is a CD buff. The size of his collection matches the inventory of some stores. He has a music room in the basement of their home where he can spend hours. He invites others to enjoy his collection with him and his family.

My friend Phyllis went for lunch. While she was in the Coal Bowl, the two aforementioned sports car testers spotted her car. They proceeded to sneak into her car. They turned up the radio full blast, turned on the windshield wipers, inter-fastened all the seat belts, changed the position of the seats, turned the name cards in all her cassette tapes backward and left a "Who Dun-It?" note on the steering wheel. Their final act was leaving lip prints on her rearview mirror!

A church secretary walked into her office. Throughout the day, behind the books, in drawers, on the telephone, in her pencil holder, in the mail drop, on the copier, in the paper rack and even by her coffee cup, she found pieces of her favorite candy.

My friend John, the CD buff, left his truck parked while he went on coffee break. To his surprise, when he returned to his truck, the entire cab was filled to the brim with styrofoam peanuts!

This is just a small assortment of some fun things I have heard and cherished because I find great pleasure in people *enjoying* life. We all have to earn a living, wash clothes, eat and take out the garbage, etc. We can let these things have the highest and only priority in our lives and spend years trudging through these duties day by day.

One of my most favorite Bible verses is John 10:10, in which Jesus says: "I am come that they might have life, and that they might have it more abundantly" (KJV). I am learning it is easy for most of us to take ourselves—and life—too seriously. Interesting, huh? I love Bruce Marchiano's portrayal of Jesus in the Visual Bible series. He portrays Jesus full of incredible, spontaneous joy, with this joy spilling onto the disciples and others around Him. In his book, *In the Footsteps of Jesus*, Bruce gives credit for some of his interpretation of a "Jesus of Joy" to a book by Sherwood E. Wirt titled *Jesus, Man of Joy*. I am reading that book now.

Maybe we need to stop now and then. Get off the imaginary treadmill we keep ourselves on. Take a break. Share a smile. Lighten the load for ourselves or someone else. Really . . . is it time you went kite flying? or walked barefoot? went wading? or got up to watch the sunrise?

There are lots of people willing to volunteer for the Moan and Groan, Gripe and Complain Committee. They don't need any more members. As a matter of fact, I think they have filled their quota.

That leaves the rest of us standing out here on the curb. Wanna' start a parade? Have a water fight? Go on a picnic? Put up a teepee? Get an ice cream cone? Have a neighborhood pot-luck?

Speaking of food, I must tell you something else. I really can't cook.

I have a sign in my kitchen that says, "Where there's smoke, there's dinner," a gift from my sons. And Robert brought home a sign from our last missionary convention and hung it over the stove. It says "Welcome to the Promised Land."

It took me fifteen years to learn to make gravy. I finally got a system. I used my old cast-iron fry pan. I'd take the meat out of the pan and then shake a certain amount of water and a certain amount of flour together in a certain yellow Tupperware container. Then I'd dump the mixture into the pan and stir it with a certain wooden spoon. Then I'd add the water from the potatoes I'd boil. Nine times out of ten, I would end up with gravy.

We lived in an apartment when we first moved to Colstrip in 1973, while we were waiting for our house to be built. I decided to really devote these first few months of living in Colstrip to my cooking. I had personal ambitions to be Colstrip's pseudo-Betty Crocker. One night, I cooked steak. I had the table set. The napkins and candles matched the tablecloth. My dress and apron complemented the color scheme. (That is the only part of cooking I like!)

When the steak was done, I took it out of my faithful cast-iron fry pan. I got my yellow Tupperware container and reached for the flour. I was out of flour! Colstrip did not have a grocery store in those days, and the nearest one was twenty-six miles away. I didn't panic. I remembered that I had that coffee can of flour I had used in our camping trailer. I rummaged through the moving boxes and found it.

Back in the kitchen, I put the certain amount of flour and the certain amount of water in the yellow container. I shook it well and poured it in the fry pan. I grabbed my certain wooden spoon and started stirring. But it was so *weird*. That gravy mixture just grabbed onto the spoon. It would not let go of that wooden spoon. I couldn't stir it. I couldn't knock it off. This had never happened before. A brown lumpish mass was hanging onto the spoon. I decided it must be the Colstrip water. Our water wasn't very good in those days, before the new town's water plant was built. So I went to the sink to refill the yellow Tupperware container. When I picked it up, the flour and water that were left in it had formed a molded copy of the Tupperware one. It fell out in the sink with a "Plink!" At that moment, a lightbulb flashed in my brain, "Oh drats!" I said.

Because now I remembered. I had been in charge of Daily Vacation Bible School in Billings the summer before. The leftover plaster of paris we had used in crafts? I had put it in a coffee can for storage!

I did the first thing that came to mind. I poured (pushed) the gravy (?) down the drain of the sink. At supper that night, I told my family that butter on potatoes was much better nutritionally. A short time later we moved from that apartment. I don't know if they ever had plumbing problems . . . I didn't ask.

# CHAPTER 7

# More Proof

I opened the refrigerator door and contemplated supper. The remains of the roast beef we had for supper on Monday were approaching death, but it could still talk. "Waste not, want not," the roast shouted at me. "A penny saved is a penny earned." And in a voice that sounded strangely like my father's, "Remember all those little starving children in Korea." My dad had served in the army in Korea. He was always reminding my brother and me of these kids at the supper table when we were growing up.

OK. OK. I took the roast out and cut it into chunks. Which was hard because it had formed a protective shell around itself—probably to protect itself from the other things in my refrigerator that are green and moving.

My friend Toni makes wonder soups and stews. "I just take everything out of the refrigerator and dump it in a pot," she told me. So I opened my refrigerator door.

OK. So the cup of corn goes in, minus the kernels on top that have petrified. The broccoli and cauliflower left from my first day of dieting, which I was going to eat on the second day of my diet, which I haven't had yet, joined the corn. I added half an onion that I had put in my refrigerator to make it smell good on the advice of Heloise. Then there was a can of mushroom soup I'd opened by mistake when I was hungry for chicken noodle. I remembered Grandma Lennemann telling me you can add mushroom soup to anything for flavor.

This definitely looked like it needed flavor. As a matter of fact, it didn't look good at all. But my Aunt Doris always says the longer things cook the better they taste. So I put a lid on the pan, turned the heat on low and went to my computer to write, praying these leftovers would get well acquainted with the roast, and this would be another marvelous invention from Lois' kitchen. I checked it from time to time and decided that's what it needed—more time.

But time eventually ran out. "What's for supper?" Robert asked as he came in the door.

"Stew-oup," I replied optimistically.

He lifted the lid. He put the lid back down. "I was thinking, maybe we should go out to eat."

"No, it will be good. It just needs a little more time."

An hour later my writing was done, he had worked out in the garage, and the conglomeration in the kettle didn't look any better.

"It's still not too late to eat out," he said. The idea was tempting but I thought about those little Korean kids.

"We'll give it some more time."

A half hour later, he lifted the lid again. I think he was hungry. "I think you should set it on the floor and see if the cats will touch it," he laughed.

"No," I said, sticking with the starving kids, "I'll just add some noodles. My mom always adds noodles to stuff."

We ate it. One helping apiece. Then Robert had bread, butter and jelly. Then he had a dish of sherbet. Then he had a couple of dishes of chocolate pudding with cream on top. I don't know if he was still hungry or just trying to kill the taste of my "stew-oup."

I reflected on it later. I could have thrown out the chunk of roast beef, cooked steak and still been money ahead. Well, maybe not money ahead, but certainly with my reputation less confirmed. The cats didn't even like it.

It was a whole chicken. With legs and wings attached. No feathers. Frozen.

The last time I dealt with a naked chicken in one piece was eons ago when we gathered at my Grandma Lennemann's for "chicken-pluckin' day." Those chickens were whole—at first. And they were hot. Grandma had a big black caldron-type kettle over a fire out in her yard filled with boiling water. It was an assembly line procedure.

There were the choppers, who cut the heads off; the dippers, who dipped the chickens into the caldron; the pluckers, who defeathered the birds; and somewhere along the line were the butchers who cleaned the insides out. Then these chickens were hauled to Grandma's freezer by all the kin on hand for the annual fete. Later, in the talented hands of my grandma, they turned into delicious dinner fare. I remember much haggling amongst us grandkids over whose turn it was for the wishbone.

The only time I ever tried to turn a whole chicken into dinner you couldn't find the wishbone. Or distinguish a wing from a thigh. Evidently there is some formula to follow in cutting the critter up into recognizable pieces.

So here I am, defrosting my freezer and here is that chicken staring me in the face. A whole chicken. It was a gift from Marilyn Vandebos. I let her keep some meat in our freezer because she didn't have enough room in her own. She had just returned from her mom's and their chicken-pluckin' day. She gave me the chicken in return for the favor.

I didn't have the courage to tell her I really preferred the cut-up variety myself. At least when I cook those, my family know they are eating a chicken. I just said "Thank you" to Marilyn and put the chicken in my freezer. Every time I go to my freezer looking for something to prepare for supper, there's that chicken. Waiting.

I really should try to cook that thing. It's getting a little tan around the edges. I was just trying to think how long I've had that bird. Let's see . . . the Vandenboses left Colstrip two or three years ago. She gave it to me a year or so before they left . . . That's a long time to sit in a freezer. Poor bird.

That's also a long time to be afraid to face the challenge of cutting up one stupid chicken. Poor me.

Maybe I can talk Grandma into coming down for a visit. We'll have chicken.

I didn't mean to burn the cauliflower a while back, either. I had gone three months without having to throw out a pan because the burnt stuff couldn't be chiseled out of it. I really thought I was getting better at this. Cauliflower is really easy. Put some water in a pan. Put the frozen block of cauliflower in the pan. Turn the stove on high. In ten minutes or so the cauliflower will be ready. My mistake was thinking I could just dash off a few lines on my computer while the cauliflower was cooking. When the smoke alarm went off I knew I had overwritten my lines!

Robert came in from the garage. He didn't miss a beat. "Sounds like supper's ready, I heard the smoke alarm."

Normally I really do pretty well. I hadn't burned anything for several weeks. Of course we had been eating out a lot. So I wasn't quite ready for my latest humiliation. I had a crying jag over the cauliflower. Then we went out to eat. The house smelled awful. I put "pan" on my shopping list for Billings.

When I came back from Bible study this afternoon, there was a message on my answering machine. I heard a friend with slight panic in her voice say, "Oh-oh-oh, you're not home. Then it doesn't matter. Well, it matters but . . . never mind, I'll tell you tomorrow."

It was late afternoon. I had to find out what the strange message meant, so I dialed her number. "This is Lois. What's wrong?" I asked.

She said, "Oh, everything's OK now. I had a fire in my oven when I called you. I had baked some pies two days ago and evidently some of the juice had spilled over. So today when I was baking some brownies, I smelled something burning. I opened the oven door and there were flames!" She said she'd tried blowing them out and even shutting the oven door. But they just kept flaming up. "I didn't know what to do," she said. "Then I thought, *Kitchen fire . . . call Lois, she'll know what to do!*"

She said when I wasn't home she went back to the blowing-it-out game plan. However, when the apple syrup got all burnt up, the fire went out.

You know, I could get really bummed out about this. But in Bible study today, we studied that lesson about being kind to our neighbors. I am glad my neighbors know they can call on me—I think. I *am* experienced with kitchen fires.

I woke up feeling wide awake, and unusually well-rested. I pulled the quilt down and opened my eyes. Sunlight streamed in through the bedroom window. That should have been cause for alarm. But the luxury of a snug bed dulled my internal alarm system.

"Lois! What day is it?" Robert sat up in bed.

"It's Thursday," I said.

"It's 7:40," he said.

The CCSC office, where I had been bookkeeper-receptionist for eight years, opened at 7:30 a.m. I was still in bed—and ten minutes late already. I was up like a shot-in-the-dark. Only now I understood the "well-rested" and "sunlight" clues! I called the office. Then in record time I made myself presentable and raced to work. It is plenty humbling walking in very late!

The next morning I jumped out of bed at the first sound of the alarm. No snooze button this morning. In the kitchen, I plugged in the coffee-pot and put a pan of water on the stove. I turned the dial to high (the only setting my stove knows; I'm always in a hurry to get out of the kitchen). I would have oatmeal for breakfast. I went back to my bathroom. I turned on my tape player to continue the "reading" of Galatians chapter 5. After bath and hair, next is face.

"I know what I'll do," I said to my face in the mirror. "I'll let Robert sleep in. He hasn't slept in one day since his retirement the end of December. After that race-gun start yesterday, he needs it." When my makeup was on, I stealthily opened our bedroom door and shut off his alarm. Then finished dressing. "It would be good if you went to work early this morning, Lois." I continued my conversation with myself. "You have some time to make up for yesterday."

At 8:30 a.m., I got a call from Robert on my office phone. "What were you cooking this morning?"

"I wasn't cooking anything . . . *oh yes, oh yes I was*! I was going to make some oatmeal!"

He told me he didn't think he could save our new, very expensive heavy Revereware saucepan. The steel plate in the bottom of the pan had separated into three pieces, he told me.

"Yikes! It's a good thing that was a good pan or the handle would have melted . . . good grief, I could have burned the apartment down!" I said. "I guess there wasn't enough water left for you to have some oatmeal?"

"Hardly!" He didn't reprimand me or call me stupid. He laughed! Bless him!

As one of my coworkers put it, "Sometimes you just have dumb weeks!"

I think I just had mine.

We were living in the apartment in Colstrip because we had just sold our house on the lake and were moving out to the country. With Robert's retirement, we found a place with a large metal building on it, perfect for his "Cars, Trucks & Parts" business he was going to start. He planned to find auto parts for people who didn't have time. I thought it was a great idea, considering his second choice was opening his own junkyard!

Larry, the man whose place we bought, needed some time to move his stuff and his mobile home off the property. In the meantime, we needed to make decisions about a home for ourselves. I wrote a poem about our place in my column:

I am not a poet, this I know,
But sometimes columns just won't flow.
   A rhyme might work and turn out right
   Or so it seems for this writer tonight.

Me and Pa, we moved north to a farm;
We get up at dawn to call of the alarm.
   We have no wheat, no fields to plow,
   We have no hay, not even a garden right now.
     I guess we don't have a farm.

Me and Pa, we moved north to a ranch,
With only ten acres, we took a chance.
   We have no sheep or hogs, only deer;
   No barn, not a bull, cow or steer.
      I guess we don't have a ranch.

Me and Pa, we moved north to a spread;
We set down a house on our homestead.
   We got the well to work and the water to run—
   Ten acres of mud and root cellar that's fun.
      But I guess we don't have a spread.

Me and Pa, we moved north to our place;
Pa retired and got out of the rat race,
   Opting into car sales for a change of pace,
   He orders parts with a smile on his face.
      I guess we got quite a place.

Ma's got a pond where ducks can swim,
A kitchen where (surprise) she's cooking for him,
   A house with a hovel where she can write,
   And beautiful sunsets to view at night.
      I guess we got quite a place.

Me and Pa, we thank God for our little place,
Where we can live at a slower pace.
   Today while Ma hung clothes out on the line,
   Pa was working on an engine whine.
      I guess we could call it "Our Place."

Later tonight, we'll both slip inside,
And sit in our chairs, side by side.
   Moonlight will bounce off the tops of old cars,
   And the pond will sparkle, mirroring the stars.

A farm? A ranch? Homestead, place or spread?
   We love it here. "Call it home," Pa said.

## CHAPTER 8

# The Olmstead Homestead

After much research, many prayers for wisdom and lots of financial discussions, we opted to buy a double-wide mobile home for our place in the country. We found that having a home built is very expensive when you are out on the prairie of southeastern Montana. From past experience we knew we couldn't tackle building anything ourselves. We'd been down that road before.

Robert had taken a day of vacation so we could finish our last fall project before winter. We had to build a twenty-four-foot cinder block retaining wall in the backyard of our house on the lake in Colstrip. Robert had helped build a cinder block building at our church camp ten years ago. That and an article about "uses of cinder blocks" were the sum total of our expertise.

On the plus side of the project, we had the foundation for the wall poured. We had the stack of blocks and the six bags of premixed mortar. We had the tools. We had each other.

On the negative side of the project, it was cold. The wind was blowing. We were in a hurry. We had to get the project done that day because of the forecasted snow. We really didn't know what we were doing. And we had each other.

If you are married, you know what I am saying.

As we worked at the project, I lovingly told him I thought he should mix the mortar a little thinner. He lovingly told me if I got the block wet on the ends, the mortar would stick like glue. The loving suggestions were soon being tossed back and forth like a game of tennis. My next line was to be, "Well, dearest, if you are such an expert, why don't you do it by yourself?" But then I remembered the trailer incident.

About eight years ago we planned a Labor Day camping trip with friends I will call, for the sake of their friendship—and their marriage—John and Jane Doe. We loaded our camping trailers and were all set to go after work Friday night.

"I can't go. The plant is going down for maintenance this weekend." The call was from my husband.

"Oh no, we've got to go," I countered. "The kids are counting on it." I thought for a minute. "I can drive the jeep and pull our trailer. After all, I am a ranch girl!" He wasn't quite as confident as I, but when I said, "We can do it. 'John' will help. We can do it," he relented. So off we went.

We got to Rock Creek campground south of Red Lodge, around midnight. "John" found a place where there were two vacant spots on each side of the road. He walked back to our jeep. "This will be perfect. Now you just drive up the road and I'll help you back the trailer in. You can do it." He gave me a reassuring smile and a pat on my shoulder. I drove up the road and started backing up. "That's it, Lois. Good job." He directed me with encouraging words, "A little to the left. Slow now. Two more feet. Watch that little bush. Good job. Cramp your wheel to the right. Great!! Now back slowly. You're doing good!" I stepped out to survey my accomplishment. The trailer was backed into the spot. We were ready to set up camp. Now it was their turn to back into the spot across the road.

"Jane" had slipped over to the driver's seat of their van. Now "John" could help her back in. "OK, drive up the road and back up slowly," he said. She started backing up, "Slow down," he yelled. "Left. *Left. Can't you hear?*" By now he was waving his arms, "THE TREE . . . STOP . . . I SAID SLOW!!! CRAMP THE WHEELS!!" He was shouting now.

I could hear every word from across the road. This couldn't be the same patient fellow who had guided me with encouragement and understanding. What was the difference between her driving and mine?

They were married.

We all laughed about it the next day (it wasn't funny the night before) and in the years since. But I have never forgotten it. The same thing would have happened to Robert and me if the tables were turned.

Robert and I stopped our work with the bricks and mortar to go into the house for a few minutes. I was freezing—in two pairs of pants and four shirts. I wanted to quit. But we were in this together—the cold, the nonstick mortar and the marriage. I said a prayer.

"I think we can do this," my husband said with confidence, as we went back outside. He put his arm around my shoulder. "We're getting the hang of it."

Later he reached over to grab the block I had just brushed off with care. His cold hand covered my cold hand. "We are doing it," he said.

I agreed. We were doing it. And we did. It was not perfect. There is a quirky little bow in the middle of the wall and some patching needs to be done. But it is our wall. We did it. The Lord and us.

Another lesson came when I was staining the back deck on that house. I did not expect it to be too difficult. It was only 130 square feet. There were one-inch spaces between each board—so not too demanding. I could do it.

I waited until afternoon so my task could be done in the shade. I was equipped for the task: a three-inch roller, a small paintbrush, my paint duds and a gallon of cedar stain. Five minutes into my job, I had a few doubts. I followed my "worst-first" edict I always use when tackling jobs. The steps and the louver side first. That would be the worst part of the deck to stain. I had to lie on my belly with my head under the stairs and do a giraffe stretch to get the boards in the corner. The small paint brush was not getting into the crevices. The thin stain was dripping to the dirt below the deck. Expensive drips. The roller would only pick up a dab from the stain can. When I rolled it down a deck board, I would get tan zebra stripes. Besides all that, kneeling on the deck was killing my knees, and I wasn't real sure I liked the color!

"Would you pick up a couple of those foam brushes on your way home for lunch?" I called Robert at work. I decided to reassess the project. I started anew. I poured some stain in a paint tray. I got a sponge pad for my knees. ("If you prayed more," a little voice convicted in my head, "you'd have tougher knees!") I got a bigger, softer brush. Robert came home for lunch and brought the foam brushes. They worked wonderfully in the crevices. I couldn't do anything about the color; I was committed now. Justin, our then-four-year-old grandson was dropped off by his dad for an hour. I let him paint with the little brush. Much sweat and three hours later, I finished the project.

The next morning I zipped out to the deck to check on my project. It looked very nice. Actually I didn't zip. My back didn't bend and my legs weren't working very well.

"I used a big paint roller with a long handle when I did ours," my mom said when we had our daily morning phone call.

"Well, that would have been smart!" I said with an "Ouch!"

There is a good lesson in this. The job didn't seem very difficult when anticipated. It was only when I got into it that I met some challenges I hadn't expected or prepared for. Compare it to marriage, raising children, being a Christian or having a job.

1. At the onset we may not be properly equipped.
2. We may have unrealistic expectations.
3. Though tools are available, we don't think we need them.
4. We think we know all we need to.

Then we have a choice. We can reassess the situation, seek the tools we need and put on our patience-duds. Or we can quit.

I am going to call it my little hill-big mountain lesson. We get prepared to climb a little hill. Once we get on the path, we realize we are climbing a mountain. That is often true in life. If I had just checked with Mom before I started—she had just done her deck—I could have saved time and my back. If I had checked out my equipment before I started, I would have saved myself stress, money and time.

I am happy though. The timing of reassessment proved valuable in my paint job. It was crucial. I didn't quit. The deck really does look good. And Justin thinks his Grammi is great because she let him paint!

Sometimes the paths of life are rough and bumpy. Quality comes when we persevere and learn along the way. Wisdom comes from admitting our problems and learning from others.

And just as my mom loves me and is glad to help, so it is with God. He has given us a Guide in the power of His Holy Spirit to help us through life's hills and mountains. I know that because He said so in His Word in John 14:17: "Even the Spirit of truth; whom the world cannot receive, because it seeth him not, neither knoweth him: but ye [believers] know him; for he dwelleth with you, and shall be in you" (KJV). And again in John 14:26, Jesus promises us that "the Comforter, which is the Holy Ghost, whom the Father will send in my name, he shall teach you all things, and bring all things to your remembrance, whatsoever I have said unto you" (KJV).

The blessing then comes when we stand on the top of the hill and realize, with God's guidance and comfort, we have conquered a mountain!

Our first move was from Bozeman, our college home, to Great Falls, Montana in 1964 when Robert went to work for the Montana Power Company. We moved all of our possessions in my dad's stock truck. Our move to the house we built on Castle Rock Lake in Colstrip in 1984 took two trips with fourteen pickups. All we needed was a band to make a real parade out of the affair! Then in the year of our thirty-fourth anniversary, we were moving again.

Our house came home. It came down the road in two parts. Miraculously, the front part fit on the back part perfectly. After two days, we did a checklist with the head put-it-together person. We shook hands and the house was ours.

I wanted to do a sleepover on the first night. But Robert didn't think we could, since we didn't have the water hooked up yet. My mom has always said she dislikes spring because that is when Dad is irrigating. "All I hear is water, water, water. We have water breakfast, lunch and supper. And we aren't just drinking it—we're ditching it."

I must take after my father. All I have thought about the last two months is water. First we had too much water. Then we had ground water running into our well. We got the well dug up and a new seal put in it. Then we had to mix bentonite to go around it. After that hole was covered up, we had to dig a water line from the well to the cistern. Next we had to locate the line from the cistern to the house. Larry hadn't used it while he lived here. Now it was lost. Well, it wasn't lost—we just couldn't find it.

Evidently it got covered up when we were digging ditches to drain the water from the spring rains which were unusually heavy this year.

We couldn't pour footings for our house until the ground was dry. Then with all the dirt work, the end of the line disappeared. So we dug and dug and prayed and dug. We even used a metal detector to no avail. Finally, He-who-takes-long-steps and is the proprietor of our new place that we call On Golden Pond decided we should activate the line. We would run water through it and hopefully water would appear at the end of the line.

It did. The water appeared in a puddle. Coming up through the floor of the garage. Evidently broken. So we trenched again. We laid a new water line.

Maybe this week Dad will have all his irrigating done and all our water problems will be resolved.

The other big news is this: the electrician and the set-your-house-up people turned on the power to our house before they left. They smelled something burning. After much checking, they discovered the source of the fire. It was in the oven. The oven broil knob was on and the range instruction book was inside in flames.

Now I have a pile of ashes in the oven. We have had our first kitchen fire—and I wasn't even cooking yet!

We gave ourselves a self-ordained edict: *Downsize*! That is easier said than done. On the floor sit boxes. The box of quilt pieces for the quilts I am going to make someday. The box of painting supplies for when I take up artwork again. My tombstone may read "Jack of all trades, master of none!" I have tried them all. A box of Native American beadwork supplies from the class I took. Inside are baby moccasins. The children for whom I was going to bead these shoes will graduate from high school before I get them done. I have cross-stitch supplies that would outfit a craft store. Some of the thread has traveled several states on vacation (just in case I might want to sit in a deck chair and do some cross-stitch). Then when you reach our age, you not only still have your children's skis and hunting vests ("Keep them, Mom—we'll want them someday!"), but you have the family heirlooms inherited from deceased family members.

And we, along with 40,000 other Americans, have every issue of *National Geographic* since 1935 (that includes my grandparents' saved issues). Who, I ask, has the guts to throw out one of those yellow-covered magazines?

I have the table that held my grandmother's Easter lily. It is missing some screws and needs refinishing. But I am not about to break the ancestral chain and throw it out. I just haven't got it fixed yet.

Then there are those misfit birthday presents. Like the hunting bow. I saved the money when it wasn't easy. I knew Robert would love a new hobby. His friend in Billings who was an avid bow hunter helped me buy the very best. Robert seemed really delighted with the gift. When he tried it out, he put a hole in the ceiling of our home in Billings. (Remember, he's 6′ 9″. ) I think that was the only time he used it. But we have been packing it around for twenty-five years because he swears it was a great gift and someday he is going to get into bow hunting!

We noticed that the more stuff we moved, the easier it was to make more trips to the dump as well. When it came time to move our big stuff, we had dear friends who volunteered, so we had another "parade of pickups."

I pray the Lord will forgive me for paraphrasing His Word. But I think this is the way John 15:13 should read: "No greater love hath any man than this, that a friend would help another *man move his stuff*" (paraphrase mine).

We taught our children not to be quitters. We learned it from our parents. We thought it was a trait worthy to be passed on. I just told you about the lesson on not quittting I learned from painting our deck. But the next week we broke that hereditarial law we had tried so hard to teach. We quit.

It was just one "ba-zillionth" raindrop that pushed us over the edge. We had moved furniture on Friday, Saturday and Monday with the help of friends. While Robert started the well pump to fill the cistern for the supreme test, I unpacked boxes. Tuesday was Independence Day. We were independently going to unload the washer and dryer, still in the back of our pickup, into our new house. That morning while still in bed, I woke up hearing raindrops. Raindrops which passed from pitter-patter to cats and dogs.

As always, He-who-takes-long-steps, the more mature partner of our home, said, "Well, we'll just have to see . . . " We drove from our nearly bare apartment out to On Golden Pond. There was mud everywhere, a sight to which we had grown accustomed.

It had turned into a mathematical formula in my brain: 2mm = 1MHTG (Too much mud equals One More Huge Truck of Gravel needed). We sat in the truck with windshield wipers singing a song we had heard one too many times. We looked at each other.

"I think now would be a good time to go on a vacation!" I said.

He said, "Good idea!" He drove the pickup down to the shop. We got a plank and unloaded the washer and dryer in the shop. We grabbed a few things from the house we had not yet slept in, and then back to town to the almost empty apartment to shower and pack.

In short order, we were back in the pickup driving the 130 miles to our "other" home. It is in the Big Horn Mountains in Wyoming. It is not a new home; as matter of fact it is an older 14 x 60 trailer home—but we feel so blessed to own it with Todd and Lisa and spend time there when we can.

A few hours later, with a few sticks of wood in the outdoor fireplace, a slightly burned but delicious marshmallow and the sight of a bull moose down in the meadow, we both gave a big sigh. Then we scooted our lawn chairs a little closer to the fire and each other.

There is a time to laugh and a time to cry, a time to plant and a time to uproot, a time for silence and a time for speech. "I think this is one of the smarter things we've done," went my little speech, a bit garbled from the marshmallow in my mouth.

"I think so too," Robert said, patting my shoulder. So for the next week we roamed the back roads of the Big Horns. Seeing God's wonderful creation in all its beauty. Spending fun time together, seeing neat sights, reading the Bible together, having quiet times and lots of conversation too. Eating steaks cooked over the campfire and hot dogs with buns that were delicious. (Robert's cooking.) And getting renewed. Maybe for once, we needed the ba-zillionth raindrop—to remind us that sometimes we need to quit—for a season!

# CHAPTER 9

# On Golden Pond

In case you ever need to know, "Oh, whoa" does not stop a lawn tractor. This writer was mowing down by the pond where the grass was long enough to bale. I was merrily mowing at high speed, singing at the top of my lungs. When I'm on our gray Sears lawn tractor, our ten acres turn into a plantation and the tractor sets off my power trip. It's at these times when I am doing this farm-type stuff that I get an invincible-woman feeling. That feeling flew away in an instant on this day. . . the instant when the steering wheel came off in my hands!

I'm now racing along on my tractor lawn mower-turned-Caterpillar diesel headed straight toward the pond—and the unattached steering wheel is in my hands! I yell, "OH WHOA!" to no avail. My horrified glance downward assured me there was not a chance of just snapping the steering wheel back on. A bolt had come off—I saw it by my feet. A panic prayer, the kind I am good at, went heavenward. That prayer caused my brain to kick in. I reached down, turning the key to off. We—the tractor and I—stopped in the cattails and mud in front of the pond!

After a "Thank You, Lord" prayer, the no-longer invincible woman went to the shop for a wrench and screwdriver. I got it fixed and proceeded on with the job at hand, at a slower speed and somewhat subdued in enthusiasm. When Robert came home, I related the incident.

"Why didn't you just stand up?" he asked, conveying all the wisdom of mechanical things that God must give to men at birth. "The engine automatically shuts off."

"In the first place, I didn't know that," I said, somewhat huffily. "Secondly, my thought was to stay in the saddle—not to try to get bucked off by standing up!"

"You fixed it, huh?"

"Yup, I did."

"You took the top off and found the nut and got it back on?"

"Yup."

"Good job!" he said and gave me a hug.

Later, he came up to the house from the shop. "That steering wheel is on there real tight now. I checked it out. You did right and it looks great."

Goodness, I love that man. I think tomorrow I might put the blade on the front of that tractor and grade some gravel. I *am* the invincible woman, you know.

Are any of you going to be wading in a river in the next few weeks and need size 7 shoes? I was just wondering. I have been cleaning my closets. It seemed like time to attack my fall cleaning. Closets were at the top of my list. I discovered I had three pairs of old, rundown tennis shoes. When my last pair wore out, I couldn't throw them away. "If I ever have to wade out after the ducks or something, I'll put these old ones on," I had said to myself. I just didn't remember I had already thought that on the previous two pairs!

The same with paint clothes. I have enough old shirts and pants that I am saving for when I paint that I could outfit an army of painters. I cannot throw away an old shirt, especially if it is flannel and has long shirt tails, my favorite. I am sure some of these work clothes I am saving are old enough to vote. They have holes in the elbows and safety pins for buttons. Why can't I throw them away?

I would like to blame my mother. She always said, "You are not going to wear those new shoes out to the barn, are you?" or "That new shirt is not for chores. You go back in the house and change into something old." So, for more than thirty years, I have been accumulating this vast storehouse of "work clothes." It would take me another thirty years to wear out my supply.

There is something special about old clothes. It must be similar to the "blankies" that toddlers drag around. When I get home from work and slip into my old, tattered, red plaid flannel shirt, I feel safe. I think I can work better when I put that shirt on too. My husband must feel the same way. Some of the outfits I have seen him in are pathetic. A bum on the rails could look better.

The minute he gets home he can't wait to put on his old Levis with holes, oil stains and fringe for a hem. You would never guess the original color of his favorite shirt that is hanging by the back door right now.

Maybe some enterprising community group should have a contest. We could all wear our favorite work clothes. They could give prizes for the oldest, hole-iest and most pathetic. We'd have a great time. We'd all feel so good and relaxed about being in our favorite outfits that the function would have to be fun. Of course it would have to be held by the river.

I have these tennis shoes I am dying to wear.

My mom is so mechanical she really can fix most anything. She can fix a fuel pump or take apart her tractor lawn mower and put it back together. She can build stuff and overhaul things. You would think that some of that might have rubbed off on her daughter, the dude. When I am trying to do something mechanical, I can hear her voice in my ear saying, "You can 'figger' anything out. There is always a way. Just use your head and think it through."

Yup. Right. My "mechanical" problem was so simple you will laugh. First, I have to tell you I opened my towel drawer in the kitchen to get a clean dish towel. "Yikes!" I said to myself, since no one else was home. "I have a mouse!"

This deduction was elementary. There were "mouse tracks" right before my eyes on the top towel. I checked under the sink. More mouse tracks. "Oh, yuck!"

I thought we had plugged up all the holes around the plumbing last year when we first moved in. I had carefully covered a small hole circling the drain under the kitchen sink with duct tape (which can fix anything). "You dirty rotten little booger!" I didn't think mice could chew through duct tape—but this one had. I knew the first thing I had to do was catch the mouse.

I got a trap out of the utility room. I got the peanut butter out of the cupboard and a plastic spoon. I put some peanut butter on the little metal do-hickey. Then I carefully put the trigger thing over the zapper thing, holding it down tightly so I wouldn't amputate my finger in the process. Try as I might, I couldn't get the trigger thing in the hole on the peanut butter bait thing. I bent it. I pulled it. I pushed it. Then I decided it must be a faulty trap. I went to the utility room and got another one. More peanut butter. More bending, pushing and pulling.

All I got was peanut butter all over the place and a sore finger. "Listen, Lois," I said to me, "you've got to be smarter than the trap." I turned it over to see if directions were printed on it. Evidently, everyone in the world knows how to set a mousetrap—there are no instructions. I got a third trap. More bending, pushing and pulling. More peanut butter. No use. I couldn't get it set.

I gave up. I washed my hands (I had peanut butter all over me). I made myself a cup of tea. (My mom also taught me you always drink tea in a crisis, right after you pray. I had not said a prayer, but I made the tea.) I would just have to wait until Robert got home and confess I was dumber than a mousetrap!

"You're kidding!" I said when he snapped the trigger deal into the slot I had slathered with peanut butter, thinking it was the bait hole. He put the trap under the sink. One hour later, we heard a "SNAP!" We had our mouse.

"No wonder we caught him so quick," I said. "The whole house smells like peanut butter!" I know that was true, because Robert reset the trap and we caught another mouse by morning. "We have to fix that space around the pipe," I told him. "Probably every mouse in the country can smell the peanut butter. They think we are a mouse restaurant!"

I called my mom. She suggested the spray insulation that comes in a can. "Cut a coffee can lid and put it around the pipe," she said. "That's what I did. Then I sprayed that goop around it . . ."

"I know, Mom, I remember . . ."

"Never mind," she laughed. "We haven't had a mouse in the house since I did all that!"

I told Robert what my mom said. He thinks when my mom says something, that's the way he should do it. She's usually right and he loves her as she loves him—lots. So we did it. No, he did it. I had given up on mechanical things for the day.

The mouse highway was sealed off. I had to sterilize all the stuff in the drawers and cupboards. You could say I have my fall cleaning done as far as my cupboards are concerned. I also won't be having a peanut butter sandwich for a while. I seem to have lost my appetite for peanut butter.

(I also want to say, if I were making mousetraps, I would put the directions on them. Not everyone is mechanically minded, you know.)

Robert and I scheduled a carpentry project On Golden Pond. We wanted to make a Christmas star. We wanted to make a big one so people driving down Highway 39 could look up on our hill and see it.

Olmstead & Olmstead, Inc., does not have a great track record. There is no Dunn & Bradstreet rating. You won't find them in the yellow pages. They are not for hire. If they were, you wouldn't want them. There is not a union. With only two employees, a union is not necessary. Besides, we both think we are the boss.

Sunday afternoon was designated as Star Project Day. (Since it was a *Christmas* star, we thought God would excuse the work on His day.) Robert got a 4 x 4 piece of plywood which we thought was perfect for the big star. The howling wind and cold weather didn't hamper our zeal. He got the power saw and an extension cord.

"OK," he said.

"OK," I said.

That's the way we start at O & O. I had the pen so I just drew one of those up and down and back and over star shapes with my black marker.

"That's not straight," he said. "The tips are not right." And they weren't. I tried it again. It still didn't look right. "Haven't you got a star we can look at?"

I tripped into the house and came out with a one-inch stuffed star from our advent calendar. He took the star without saying a word. Then he took the pen and he tried. Then I tried. Then he tried. Next I went into the house to get some other color marking pens. It was getting difficult to tell which line was the new "right" line. We tried straight lines with a yardstick. Then we tried a newspaper triangle hinged on a pizza pan circle in the middle. Finally the O & O engineering manager went in to his desk and got a protractor, compass and some other mechanical thing. He drew a right-reasonable star. The board was plaid from all the lines running across it. He had done his latest attempt in purple and managed to follow it with the saw. We stapled the lights on it. The wind was blowing too hard to put it on our utility pole. Besides, it was too dark also.

"We did that whole project and didn't get mad. Isn't that great?" I commented. He agreed. However, we both knew the fact that our precious grandson, Justin, who was helping us, was probably the only reason the markers and the lopsided star weren't in the pond by then.

Robert called me at work on Monday. "Be sure to look for the star as you come home. I got it up on the pole." I couldn't wait to see how it looked from the highway.

I found out we needn't have worried about the shape of our star. If you are driving on the highway during the Christmas season, look to the west just before milepost 32. Really look. You can see our big star to the west. It looks kinda like a tiny mass of red reflectors. On second thought, you better bring binoculars.

Sewing falls into the construction category also. Shirts, pants, suits, shorts and jackets—I sewed them all for our family in our early days. I sewed out of a love for sewing. I also sewed out of necessity. Two of us going to college put a hole in our already empty pockets. The wages from Robert's summer job running power plants in Yellowstone Park had to last all year. Fabric was cheap by today's standards: patterns were 75 cents each. So I made our clothes. As the baby boys came, I made their clothes too. Later I taught sewing lessons to women in small Montana towns to aid our income. There weren't many tall men's stores in those days either. My 6-foot, 9-inch husband wore homemades. I had to alter the patterns to fit him.

One day I spent many hours on a long-sleeved plaid dress shirt. I made sure the plaids on the pockets, yokes and cuffs all matched. It was a real labor of love. But love was a slender thread when he tried it on and the sleeves were too short! Naturally I cried first. (Do young brides still cry lots, I wonder?)

I had to put all the skill I could muster, with many prayers, into fixing the shirt. I pieced a three-inch strip of the few scraps of precious material I had left into each sleeve, painstakingly matching every stripe. When he came home from classes, I said, "Try it on now."

He went into the bedroom to change. When he came out, the cuffs of the shirt were three inches above his wrist! "Oh, no!" I couldn't believe it. But before the tears came, my darling husband grinned—and pulled the sleeves down from where he had carefully folded them at his elbows!

Now after being married to him for thirty-eight years, I would expect him to play a joke like that. Back then I was fair game for all of his shenanigans.

This week I have a great opportunity to get even. I told him mending was the last to-do on my February list. "Would you get out everything that needs to be fixed?" I asked one night after work. He brought me two pairs of tan Dockers.

"I'll try them on so you can see what needs fixing." He stood in the living room modeling Pair One. They were too short. "Can you let the hem out?"

"I think so. What's wrong with the other pair?" I waited for him to slip into Pair Two.

"See. They are too long. I've never worn them. Can you shorten them up?" said the loving husband of the old sleeves-too-short trick.

"Sure, no problem," I said. All I have to do is make the short pants shorter and the long pants longer. I think God will forgive me, don't you?

Easter is being heralded in Colstrip and we are not talking about the weather. It is pageant time. Over 100 people work on bringing the realistic drama to life on Palm Sunday weekend each year. This is the fifth annual Easter Pageant, sponsored by the First Baptist Church. People from every church in town participate, making it a real community event. Work on the pageant starts months in advance as the script is re-written each year and new sets and costumes are added.

This year I'm helping with the wardrobe. (One year in the nursery necessitated volunteering for the choir and *anything* else rather than doing that again!)

"We need new soldier skirts this year," Karen Woods, pageant director, told me.

"I can do that," I said. Robert went with me when we drove the two-hour trip to Billings to scour the fabric shops for soldier skirt material.

"Look at this," he said.

"It's perfect!" I said. "It looks like it just came off a camel train en route to Rome! Let's get it! Good find!" The fabric was a heavy denim that looked like it had been sprayed with gold glitter. It had a metallic look. I couldn't wait to get at sewing it.

The next day I began putting the design in my head to work on the fabric. I made a dropped-waist girdle, fastened with brass snaps. Then I fashioned the knee-length skirt. "You guys probably don't remember this," I said to my sewing buddies in the basement of the Baptist church where we had set up shop. "We used to sew creases in our Levis just like this. We wouldn't have thought of wearing them without the one-eighth-inch creases sewn down the front of the leg!" Naturally, no one did remember those.

After I got the creases sewn every three inches on the skirt, I formed triangular points at the hem. I put a brass paper fastener at each point, carefully folding under the prongs. Then I attached the skirt to the girdle top. It looked excellent! "I bet Caesar would have ordered some of these," I said to my coworkers. There was one man working at the church that afternoon on the furnace, but I didn't have the nerve to ask him to try on my "designer-soldier skirt." I took it home with me.

"Drop your pants, please," I said to Robert as soon as I walked in the door. "I want you to try on my soldier skirt." The man is such a saint. Five minutes later he was standing in the middle of our living room clad in his Car Quest shirt (his new part-time job) and the gold metallic soldier skirt.

"Oh, it looks so good! It's perfect!" I said, dancing around him in our living room.

Somewhat reluctantly, he said, "There is one problem . . ."

"Like what?" I asked, stopping my dance.

"I can't walk."

He demonstrated. He could only take baby steps. We both started laughing. We laughed at the picture of the Roman soldiers taking baby steps up the aisle at the pageant. They would be resplendent in their brass chest armor, shields, spears, gold wristbands and tall gold helmets with red feathers. They just couldn't march! "It reminds me of that song, 'Walk, Don't Run' that was popular in the '50s," quipped Robert.

"Hold still," I said. "I'll get the scissors." Now he was really scared. But a few slits up the creases of the gold skirt fixed the problem—and even made it look more authentic.

"I hope they have something to wear under this thing," said the ever-modest man whose white legs are never seen in public.

"Oh they do. They have a red skirt under it and red shorts under that."

As he went to the bedroom to take off the skirt, I heard him still laughing. I thought he was probably thinking how fortunate he is to be playing Joseph of Arimathea in the pageant. (He calls himself "Joseph of Armell's Creek.") Wearing that ankle-length dress won't seem half so bad now. Really, he was thinking of an army of Roman soldiers baby-stepping their way to victory in tight, high-fashion gold metallic skirts with labels that say, "Fashioned by Lois on Golden Pond!"

We thank God every day for the joy of living On Golden Pond. The second year on our place, we decided to get some different varieties of ducks, not just mallards. Now it was really heaven-on-earth for me. Our grandchildren loved coming out to visit. Friends dropped in often for coffee and to enjoy the ducks.

"Robert, how many ducks did you count yesterday?"

"Fifteen, why?"

"Because I only saw twelve just now. The others must have been hiding."

"That's strange," he said. "They never stray very far from each other. Let's go down to the pond and look again." Twelve ducks came when we called. They eagerly ate the pieces of bread from our hands as we recounted.

"That Cayuga female and one mallard are not here," I said.

"And Bubba's gone!" said Robert. We had both become very attached to this big blue-and-gray duck. Just then our friends Karen and Eldon dropped in. They walked around the pond with us looking for the missing ducks or signs of a struggle, like feathers, hoping both to find and not find any. Eldon even walked down the road to the smaller pond that is on our place.

"They just wouldn't leave each other to go that far," I told Eldon. "They stick together."

"I wonder what could have got them . . . and us not hear a ruckus?" Robert said.

I was surprised at just how bad I felt. We knew there was danger with foxes, coyotes, dogs and who-knows-what out in the country. But this group of ducks was so fast and so skittish that we felt they would be safe. Especially Bubba. "Maybe you should call the State Fish and Game about setting up a trap," suggested Eldon. We discussed penning them up every night.

"Oh, yes, like they are about to go back in the pen after being free?" Robert laughed. "That would be a real circus watching that . . ."

Throughout the evening, one of us would go down to the pond and count the ducks. Still twelve. At 10 p.m. I asked Robert what we should do. "You can bet whoever had a big fat duck for supper last night will be back for more," I told him. "I guess we could stay up all night and watch." He looked at me. "Just for tonight—to see if IT comes back."

Being the night owl in our marriage, he took the first watch from 10:00 p.m. until 2:00 a.m. Then he woke me up. "There are still twelve ducks. I am going to bed if you're sure you don't want me to stay up with you."

My pioneer roots were offended. "I will be fine," I said. He handed me his super-heavy-duty deluxe saved-under-the-bed-for-who-knows-what flashlight. He rolled into bed with a big yawn. "Wake me up if you see anything."

In two minutes I could hear him snoring as I got the flashlight and parked my chair at our front window: duck guard reporting for duty. But my view was not real clear. The "hippie wagon" he was parting out blocked my view. "I know what I'll do," I said to myself as I grabbed my coat and the flashlight. "I'll go sit in the hippie wagon! My very own stakeout. Then I can see better."

There was a seat left in the green and white VW van. It had been carpeted top to bottom. Part of the floor was gone. I could see grass where the engine and gears used to be. Other than the noises of the ducks swimming around in the pond and an occasional "Croak" from a frog, I didn't hear anything. An hour into my stakeout I decided (I had a lot of time to think) that a coyote or a fox could not have captured three ducks without a trace. The coyotes and foxes we have seen on our place traveled alone. One could not have killed three ducks without noise. "So, Lois, what could it have been?" It was dark. I could only see shadows from the yard light up by our house.

Suddenly, my brain got a new thought. *A mountain lion! That's what it was! Yup, it could knock three ducks over in one swipe. Todd said there were several sightings of a mountain lion down on the Broadus ranch. I will just bet it was a mountain lion.* My mind ran right down that path, which was made easier by my being up in the middle of the night and alone in the dark. The next thought was, *OK, what if it comes back . . . and I'm sitting here with the Grand Canyon wide open under this seat . . . I could scream all night. Robert would never hear me.*

*I wonder how mad he would be if I pounded on the side of his hippie wagon with his A-1 flashlight to get his attention?* Nope, couldn't do that.

I didn't last too much longer. The shadows got darker. Shapes kept appearing and then turning back into the trees and bushes that they were all along. The noises got louder. Now my head was turning like a top, trying to keep every hill and gully in my view.

"This is *enough!* I am done," I said to the ducks. "You are on your own. If you are smart as you should be, you will stay in the middle of the pond."

After a careful look around, scanning every shadow, I stepped out of the van. My heart rate was at tourist-highway-speed. I couldn't run to the house because, of course, I had to watch for an errant rattlesnake. (We had never seen one by the pond, but my mind was filled with dangerous animal categories.) But I also had to get to the house before the mountain lion got me. It was the ultimate power-walk. Just as I got to the driveway, I saw two big eyes blink in the glare of the flashlight!

My next step took me from the driveway to the top of our porch in one giant leap. I skipped the three steps as unnecessary. I was so scared I couldn't even scream, for which Robert later thanked me. I turned the flashlight back on the eyes from the safety of the porch. It was not a mountain lion—just a big old fat bullfrog. But it sure looked like a mountain lion!

I had enough adrenaline to stay up the rest of my shift, watching over the ducks from the front window, until the sun broke over the hills.

The next morning the man I live with said, "I will tell you right now, we are not doing that every night. Those ducks are on their own."

I told him I thought he was probably right.

## CHAPTER 10

# And Then
# There Were Ducks

This new addition to our lives first came while we were living in Colstrip on Castle Rock Lake Drive: What travels in a pack, consumes 150 pounds of food in three weeks and drinks more water than a dishwasher? My ducks.

Seeking a new adventure, I decided to get baby ducks. I ordered them from the Forsyth Seed company. I didn't know how many to order but eighteen seemed like a good number. Then I went home to enlist my husband's engineering experience in building their home. We used a borrowed rabbit hutch for their house. It took fifty feet of chicken wire to enclose the pen totally. I bought waterers and feeders. I even added a covered patio.

They arrived at the post office. You could hear them peeping through the little round holes in the box. There were twenty-two fuzzy brown ducks. There must have been some twins. The pen seemed awfully big when I put them in. Ducks stick together. I mean really together.

Wherever they go, it is in a pack. The little fuzzy pack runs to the water—together. Then they run to the food—together. If one lies down, they all lie down. When one gets up, they all get up. It's like one moves and the others say, "That's a good idea!"

I did not realize how time-consuming being the ducks' stepmom would be. They are always out of water or food. And since it has been raining for two weeks, the pen requires constant cleaning.

I hadn't thought about getting up at 6 a.m. to slosh out in the rain to feed my adventure. Or going down to the lake when it's dark to get another pail of water.

I took three of them to Mrs. Berube's kindergarten class for show and tell. I won't write the details but we used lots of paper towels! They are going to Vacation Bible School at the Alliance church. Then I will turn them loose on the lake. I sure hope they can swim. If they can't, I guess I can write a column about swimming lessons for ducks.

You know, in some ways they are like people. What one does, they all do. I really think if one ran into a dog's mouth, they all would follow. It has been a good lesson. But I learned a bigger lesson from this adventure. When I was little I begged for a rabbit. My parents finally gave in. I had Bugsy two weeks before reality sunk in. Bugsy was *work.* Rabbit cages are not fun to clean. When I sold him after the 4-H County Fair, I was not sad.

You would think after all these years I would be smarter.

Ducks are cute. And having more mallard ducks on the lake will be nice. But cleaning the duck pen . . . ugh! They are not self-cleaning. They require food and water about six times a day. I keep reminding myself how much I wanted them—and Bugsy. My dad called this morning to tell me that his neighbor has two cute little baby pigs for sale.

No, I guess one adventure this month is enough.

*June 5, Friday, 5 p.m. All systems go. Preparing for launch. Weather clear.* I stepped into the duck pen. My contamination suit consisted of old clothes, tennis shoes and gloves. I forgot a face mask. Ick.

The ducks quacked wildly and ran. They did not want "Mom" in their house. I caught the ducks one at a time and handed them to Robert, who put them in a dog show pen. It is hard to catch twenty-two ducks, one at a time, and not take a breath. Ick. When the last one was caught, I stepped from the maternity pen with applause from those invited to the Duck Launching Party. We then walked the dog show pen down to the small pond behind our house.

I need to explain here that I had decided that I could not launch my ducks into the big lake as previously planned. Castle Rock Lake is a 180-acre man-made lake formed with water piped from the Yellowstone River thirty-four miles north. The water is used for the steam-generating plants in Colstrip. We natives call it the "surge pond" unless we are trying to impress someone that we live on a lake in southeastern Montana. The lake is a big place. Who knows what might happen to my babies out there.

So they were being launched into a small backwater pond right behind our house. You have heard the expression "as a duck takes to water"? It is true. They hit the water with a splash. They quacked. They splashed. They dove. They swam. (No lessons either!) We took their pen apart and pulled their house down in the trees by the lake. We cleaned up the area where the pen had been. Then we served iced tea and watched the happy ducks. The launch was a success.

*June 5, Friday, 9 p.m.* I looked out the window. The ducks were in a huddle. They were standing in the bare spot where their pen had been. Quacking. I was in my nightgown. Robert held the flashlight and did not complain as I talked and coaxed the ducks. We showed them where their house was now. They didn't seem satisfied but Robert convinced me they should be all right. I had him turn our redwood picnic table over by the little pond as a pond-side shelter.

I was up at the crack of dawn to check my babies. They came the minute I opened the back door and followed me as I got their breakfast and fed them. Then they ran for the little pond for another dip. In the days following, I watched them for hours. They followed me around the yard. They ate from my hand. They slept under our deck. They performed for guests.

But I knew I had to let them go to the big surge pond. The first time we herded them down to the lake, they were back in two minutes. I kept moving their feeder further from the house. We had a near crisis one day when I ran out of duck food. But I checked my pantry, decided on Grape Nuts, and that sufficed while I made another thirty-seven-mile run to Forsyth Seed Company for more duck food.

*Friday, June 12, 7 a.m.* This morning when I went out to feed them, they were swimming in the lake. They came when I called and ate with gusto . . . and then ran for their new swimming pool. When I went out with their lunch I couldn't see them. I called but they did not come.

*Friday, June 12, 5 p.m.* We went out in the canoe and found them down at John Williams' fraternizing with his ducks and geese. I called to them. They followed us home. But the minute they finished eating, they headed back to their newfound friends. I think my ducks have grown up. I didn't realize cutting the apron strings would be so difficult.

I fed a box of All-Bran to my ducks this morning. Not because I thought they needed it, but because it had been in my cupboard for over two years. I had watched a program on TV on healthy diets for people over forty, so I went right down to the store and stocked up on high-fiber foods. I was going to eat a bowl of All-Bran every morning.

After I fed the ducks, I decided to check my pantry for other groceries that had lived with our family a long time. The oldest residents were six quarts of dill pickles that I canned in 1976. We opened one jar the first fall. Robert took one bite and gagged. I said, "Maybe they haven't aged long enough."

The next year I opened another jar. I needed pickles to take to a potluck dinner and forgot to buy any. Robert said, "You aren't going to take *those* pickles, are you?" So I tasted one. I took carrot sticks to the potluck dinner and put the jar of pickles in the refrigerator. After several months in the refrigerator, the pickles went in the garbage. Every time I clean my pantry—or move (both usually occur simultaneously and only then) I see the six remaining jars of pickles. I wonder if ducks like pickles?

I have seven boxes of pistachio Jell-O instant pudding mix. A few years ago I went to a party where the hostess made this delicious dessert with pistachio pudding. I got the recipe. When I went grocery shopping the next time, I thought of that good dessert and bought a package of the mix. But I never got around to making it. A few months later I had to furnish the dessert for a shower. I decided I'd make the pistachio dessert and bought two boxes of the mix. But my schedule got hectic and I ordered a cake from the bakery instead. I picked up a couple boxes when I did all my holiday grocery shopping last year. I was in a real baking mood. But then I couldn't find the recipe. Does anyone have a dessert recipe that calls for seven boxes of pistachio pudding mix?

I also have four cans of Old El Paso refried beans. I was going to have Karen and Eldon Woods over for Indian tacos before they left for Texas. Let me think. Was that three years ago they moved?

There is a box mix for egg foo yung. When we went on vacation last year, my cousin in Boulder, Nevada had us over for supper. She served a fantastic meal of different Chinese dishes. I copied all the recipes. But when I got home, I saw this box mix in the store and thought I would start with it. It says, "Just add eggs." However, I never seem to get the right menu together that goes with it. Tonight we are having hot dogs . . . and egg foo yung?

I have other antique groceries. At my wedding shower everyone brought a can of spices. I have caramon, turmeric and sweet basil leaves if you ever need to borrow some. Also a box of whole dill weed from when I made the pickles in '76. There are two cans of Watkins Dessert Mix that have never been opened. I have both banana and butterscotch flavors. Last year I discovered Colstrip had a "Watkins Man." I called him right away and asked him to come over. I think Watkins Horse Liniment is the absolute best thing in the world for muscle aches. My jar (a collector's item now) was about gone. As I looked through his catalog I saw the Dessert Mix. My mom always used that to make pies when I was growing up. They were absolutely the best pies! My favorites were banana and butterscotch.

"Will the ducks fly south this fall?" That is the big question around our house lately. Everyone has a different opinion. One person told me that mallard ducks raised as domestic ducks will never fly south. So I trotted right down to the library. I got two books on ducks. One book told me how to build a hutch or coop. And how they mate. I read how to prepare a duck for roasting, ugh. I think not!

The other book, "Peg-Leg Pete" was written by a wildlife columnist in Michigan. His home was surrounded by small ponds. He had several mallard ducks. One duck got his foot caught in a trap. Pete's foot was amputated on the kitchen table with the whole family watching the procedure. They put a bandage on the foot and placed Pete in a box in the basement. With much love and care from the author's two young daughters, Pete survived the amateur operation. The book chronicles the life of this family and the duck. Peg-Leg Pete flew south about ninety miles to a warm water lake with the other mallard ducks in the fall. They knew this because the author had written about Pete in his column. One of the readers spotted a one-legged duck. The family packed a lunch and made the trip south to see if it was really Peg-Leg Pete.

I can relate to that. These ducks become part of the family. I step out on our deck and call, "Hi, ducks." They answer by quacking loudly. I feed them a bucket of mixed wheat and corn early in the morning. I stand down by the lake calling, "Here, ducks," and immediately from across the water they race toward breakfast.

They eat out of my hand. They let me pet them or pick them up. I told Robert I was going to quit feeding them more than once a day so they can get toughened up in case they do fly south. But then someone stops at our house to see them. I can't resist . . . a little more corn or one more slice of bread. The kids—and the ducks—love it.

My husband and I were going out in the canoe every evening. I would call the ducks and they would go along. They paddle behind us while we go across the lake. We made it a point to detour around fishermen who might not appreciate our noisy entourage.

Now I have great news. I talked to a nurse whose father-in-law has ducks. I learned from him about duck races in a city in New Mexico. The first prize is $5,000. He is going to send me information.

This morning when I went to feed them, I stood right at the edge of the water and called. They were swimming by some bushes about 200 yards away. I couldn't help rating their speed as they swam to breakfast. I gave the winners, I mean the first ducks, a big handful of corn. I am not seriously considering this New Mexico duck race thing at all. However, as I walked back to the house, I was thinking about the demolition derby at the County Fair. "Time Out With Lois" was painted on the rear fender of one of the cars. I paid to be a sponsor.

Oh, I know. Paint won't stick to duck feathers.

I sat out by the lake this morning for my devotions. The ducks were all around me. I found some interesting verses in Jeremiah 18. They say,

> This is the word that came to Jeremiah from the LORD: "Go down to the potter's house, and there I will give you my message." So I went down to the potter's house, and I saw him working at the wheel. But the pot he was shaping from the clay was marred in his hands; so the potter formed it into another pot, shaping it as seemed best to him.
>
> Then the word of the LORD came to me: "O house of Israel, can I not do with you as this potter does?" (8:1-6)

I am so glad that God does not give up on us. I am thankful that His mercy is for everyone. The Bible is full of verses that tell of God's love for mankind. And how Jesus died on the cross for our sins.

We had relatives visit from California this summer. They took our picture with a disposable camera. The film and camera are one. When you buy your next roll of film, you just buy another camera. We have disposable diapers and disposable razors, disposable dishes and disposable medical supplies. The slogan for today is "Use it and throw it away."

In studying the Old Testament and the history of the nation of Israel this summer, I saw that they would trust God and then they would turn their backs on Him. They would get in trouble and then yell for help . . . from God, of course. And He would answer their call. Many times they suffered the consequences of their deeds, but God never gave up on them. Jeremiah 31:3-4 says, "I have loved thee with an everlasting love: therefore with lovingkindness have I drawn thee. *Again* I will build thee" (KJV, emphasis mine). He could have easily said, "I am done with you. I have had enough. You are never going to get it right!"

But He didn't. And He didn't give up on David. He didn't give up on Peter. And He does not give up on us either. God says, "I will never leave thee, nor forsake thee" (Hebrews 13:5, KJV), and in another verse, "Cast all your anxiety on him because he cares for you" (1 Peter 5:7).

I stop to talk to the ducks for a while. Then I tell God I have some friends who are going through some rough times. I am sure they are not the only ones who are being plagued with illness and financial woes and family difficulties. But I know God knows. He does not dispose of us when we falter or have difficulties. As I continue to pray for my friends, I am reminded of the verse that says He takes the marred clay in His hands and makes it into a new vessel. I am sure that clay pot yells, "Ouch!" a few times as it spins around the potter's wheel—and so do I. But what peace there is in believing that the "Potter" knows best. "Thou wilt keep him in perfect peace, whose mind is stayed on thee" (Isaiah 26:3, KJV).

The ducks have gone to the lake for a swim. I grab my coffee cup, Bible and lawn chair and head back to the house. This "pot" is ready for the day.

"I am tired of reading about your ducks," said my dad.

"Please, Lois, no more stories about your ducks," said my editor.

So this is not a column about my ducks. This is about some other ducks. I got the information on the Great American Duck Races in Deming, New Mexico. The good news is that the prize really is $5,000. The bad news is that the races started August 23. We missed it!

This is a big event. They publish a newsletter about competitors and sell T-shirts, bumper stickers and caps. They have produced a video "duckumentary" of the contests. The races have drawn an estimated

47,000 spectators in the last five years. The ducks are placed separately in eight sixteen-foot long tracks enclosed with "duck" wire.

The ducks' coaches are allowed to run along narrow tracts atop the cages, shouting encouragement at the little quackers. The competition is tough. The contest started in 1980 with 182 webbed contenders and grew to 400 title hopefuls in 1986. Some of the competitors have been Count Duckula, Sir Francis Drake, Deputy Duck and Jake the Drake. The most important rule, according to the Official Rule Book, is that ducks are not to be mistreated at any time.

The town of Deming goes all-out for the event. There is a Duck Downs Balloon Race, Best Dressed Duck Contest, Duck Queen Contest and a Duck Parade. The weekend activities culminate with The Great American Duck Ball.

I appreciate Howard Vassau getting the information to me. He has ducks also. I heard this week that a family in Colstrip has ducks that jump off a two-foot ledge into a kiddie wading pool, then waddle around to the ledge and dive in again. Maybe our local County Fair should contact the officials in Deming. We could have Divisional Duck Races. This could really get big. Next would be World Duck Olympics.

When I send for the duck video from Deming, I am going to order one of their bumper stickers. It says I love my you-know-whats with a picture of one. I should order two more. I could give one to my dad and one to my editor.

# CHAPTER 11

# And Then There Were More Ducks

I knew I couldn't keep thirty-nine ducks safe and warm through the hard Montana winter that was forecast (by the length of beaver hair, bark on trees, depth of grass roots and *The Farmer's Almanac*). My flock had grown with donated ducks. (Seems Easter cuddly ducks are wanted only briefly. Reminds me of Bugsy!) I would need a heated duck house of considerable size. I would have to build it, get electricity wired in and figure out a water system.

My other alternative would be extension cords and my blow dryer. I would be lakeside thawing the ducks out of the ice. I must admit Robert had to listen to lots of my concern and stewing about what I was going to do. So I should not have been surprised when he said, "A man wants to get twenty of the ducks. He can come Thursday."

"My ducks? Why?"

"He raises ducks, rabbits and geese. He heard about yours. I knew you were worrying about them." I knew my husband was right. I knew I had to do something. I also knew I did not like the idea of giving them away and I wasn't sure if I liked my husband either, just because he suggested it.

I worked my way through the decision. I would do it this way: eleven of the ducks belonged to my neighbor, John Williams. Because they are also mallard ducks, we don't really know which were originally John-ducks and which were Lois-ducks. So I told myself the man could have John's eleven ducks. Then three of the white ducks that were dropped off here do not have leg bands. That would leave only six of "my" ducks having to go.

The man came on Thursday. He had a pickup with a metal stock rack. I told him to drive down by the lake where I feed them every day. I took my food and camera and went to call the ducks. I felt like Benedict Arnold. They came like always. I fed them in a holding pen and then started picking out the to-go-ducks.

We had had to cut a fishhook out of Willard's leg last June; he barely survived. He couldn't go. Chester limps from a fishhook injury. He couldn't go. Peepers and Squeakers are white ducks that came from two little girls in Billings. They couldn't go. One duck gave such a fight when I was carrying him from the pen to the pickup that I decided he should get to stay. I let him loose. I kept enough hens so I could have equal opportunity if they mated in the spring. I finally had twenty ducks in the pickup.

I wasn't very kind to the man, either. I had convinced myself he was going to "wring their necks" as soon as he got home and serve them at a banquet. He told me he was going to put them in his garden and they'd have lots of food there. He was very nice. I was not.

All I could see in the pickup box were seventeen little green heads and three little white heads bobbing up and down as he drove away.

"They are ducks. Just ducks, Lois," I said to myself as I walked back to the house with tears running down my face. "Just ducks."

Dear Sir:
I didn't catch your name. But I have been bothered since Thursday about my attitude toward you. I wasn't very nice. You were solving my problem—that I really didn't want solved. I apologize to you.
Sincerely, Lois

Dear Robert:

I am sorry about the cold, silent treatment. We lost two precious days of our relationship because I was pouting. I'm sorry.

Lois

"Just ducks."

I spent some time sitting on a rock down by the lake this last week. The ducks came the minute they saw me leave the house. They quacked loudly and looked in my pockets for food. I gave them a few handfuls of corn, which they quickly devoured. Then they waddled to the lake to play.

I am thankful for the ducks. They are walking, feathered illustrations of human nature. They have brightened my life. They can be so funny. And lots of children have enjoyed meeting them too. As I sat on the rock, I told God how thankful I am that He loves me. My favorite Bible verse is John 10:10: "I am come that [you] might have life, and that [you] might have it more abundantly" (KJV). I am so thankful for my family. My husband has been my best friend, my support, and has encouraged me to be all God wants me to be. Our sons have blessed our lives. There have been good times and bad times, but they taught us how far love will stretch . . . and how to trust God. And they even ate my cooking!

I am thankful for our parents. My parents gave me a rich Christian heritage and a solid love base by trusting God themselves. George and Cora Olmstead raised their son to be the man I fell in love with years ago. I so appreciate our daughters-in-law and our grandchildren. I am so thankful for this year. It has been a year of learning. Learning to be vulnerable in relationships. Learning about a deeper commitment to prayer and growing with God. It has been a year of new friends and opportunities. I experienced serious illness for the first time in my life this year and learned about trusting God with my life in a new way. Many times I trusted and prayed when I didn't feel like it. But God was always faithful. I learned all about stick-to-itiveness. *Thank You, God, for making my life "abundant."* I guess it's time to get off my rock. It's getting cool outside. Thanksgiving is approaching.

No one told me that I should give my ducks ice skating lessons as part of their upbringing. I prepared for cold weather. A rancher friend gave me eight bales of straw. I covered an old rabbit hutch with plywood and hauled it down by the edge of the water. I put the straw bales around their house. The level of the lake is raised in the winter so that there will be enough water for use in the Montana Power generating plants. I had forgotten about that. I ended up moving my ducks' winter resort three times so it wouldn't be underwater.

My friend Nona fed my ducks while we were at the ranch for Thanksgiving. When I got home there was a note on the cupboard. "Dear Lois: Your ducks do not like the ice. You are going to have to teach them to ice skate during your spare time this week. Invite me over when you do it. I want to watch. Love, Nona."

I grabbed the feed bucket and ran down to the lake. I called the ducks. They quacked loudly (they were glad I was back—I could tell) and swam toward our house. But the ice formed a barrier about twenty-five feet from shore. They swam back and forth quacking in distress. No amount of cajoling on my part would induce any of the nineteen ducks to jump up on the ice. I flapped my arms yelling, "Fly, you dummies. That is what you are ducks for!"

But the insults didn't faze them. They finally swam back to the north side of our cove on the lake. I poured the wheat and corn onto the ground by the vacant duck house in case they got brave when I left. That night I related the events to Robert, "I guess I will just have to walk out on the ice and lay their food out on the edge."

He said, "Well, that ice better get a whole lot thicker than it is now if you are going to attempt that!" I ignored the implications of that remark and asked him to come down to the lake and help me get feed to the ducky darlings. We walked up the edge of the lake to where the water was deeper. The ducks could swim right to the bank. Then with me in the front with the feed bucket and Robert in the back, we walked-waddled the ducks on the path back to our house.

They ate with gusto. I wanted them to walk back down the path so they get the idea that they had alternative routes to the lake. But when they finished eating they started across the strip of ice to the open water. They fell, they slid, they flapped their wings for balance and coasted with a splash into the lake. The next day we repeated the trek. The wild ducks fly onto the ice and come right up to Duck Haven (that's what I named the winter house). They have no problem with the ice. I told my ducks to watch those ducks.

I am beginning to feel like a failure as a stepparent. My ducks don't fly well, and now they can't ice skate. If my diet and exercise program doesn't produce results soon, I won't be able to walk on the ice. We could be in a terrible fix this winter. A friend suggested I glue sandpaper to their feet. I think he was kidding.

Robert said, "Did you see this?" He handed me the want-ad section of the newspaper pointing to an ad that read: Live ducks for sale. $3 each. Contact Forsyth Country Club.

"Yup, I saw it," I said.

"How could they sell those ducks for $3?" he asked.

"Well, I don't know how they could even 'sell' them in the first place," I said. "Seems similar to selling babies if you ask me."

"They sure must know something we don't," he said.

"What do you mean?" I asked.

"Well, it just must be a sign of the times," he said.

"What?"

"When you start selling $90 ducks for $3," he said.

I gulped. Changing the subject was out of the question. "Maybe they have lower-class ducks," I said.

There was silence from his corner. I knew he was thinking twenty-two ducks times $1.85, thirty feet of chicken wire, two sheets of plywood, two poultry waterers, one duck feeder, one blue plastic garbage can for feed, one heat lamp. "How much feed have you bought?"

I knew God was listening. "Just 2,850 pounds," I said truthfully. I hoped he would not ask how many trips to Forsyth Seed Company thirty-seven miles away.

"Let's see, it comes in fifty-pound bags, you get it one or two bags at a time . . ."

"Just a minute," I said. I knew I better do some fast talking. "Remember four of those ducks were free because I ordered eighteen and they sent twenty-two."

"That's $7.40," he said. I was glad he didn't mention the vet. I had to take Chester to the vet with his bad leg.

"And then there was that trip to the vet and Chester's medicine," he said.

"What can I say? Maybe they just don't take this duck-raising business seriously. Maybe they get donated food. Or maybe they got a government grant to subsidize their duck production."

His eyes brightened. "You think there is a grant possible?"

138

"I'm sure I could write to the White House and ask about that. When you consider the aesthetic benefits of happy ducks swimming cheerfully on otherwise drab ponds of water and the happiness they bring to children's hearts when they get to feed real live ducks, not to mention the educational benefits . . ." My mind was racing. I was on a roll. "Not to mention grasshopper control. Why, we could even start a National Duck Association and have conventions," I said.

"Sure," he said, "and then we could have flight tickets and duck travel cages and motel bills and vet-assistants to travel with your entourage."

"Maybe I better not write the White House."

"Good," he said.

"Really, if they are selling their ducks for such a low price, maybe I should just call that number . . . "

"No, I think not," he said. I agreed.

Winter update. As the lake froze over in December, the ducks kept a hole open in the ice of the lake. Many wild ducks joined them. Even as the depth of the lake ice got to eighteen inches, they were able to keep a large area open by swimming around it day and night. I wondered if they were on shifts: "OK, you paddle the night shift. I'll just sit on the sidelines and sleep." The ducks were industrious and never slacked off, but the edges of the ice crept inward in spite of their efforts. The little open space kept shrinking a few inches each day.

They did learn to ice skate. I would call them. They would fly up on the ice and waddle toward me. The more they hurried, the more their feet would slip out from under them. It would have made a delightful video to film them coming across the ice with Skater's Waltz playing in the background. They finally realized that their wings were useful.

They would flap furiously, flying clumsily ten inches above the ice. When they got close to me, they'd hit the ice, skidding for several feet. The more they practiced, the more graceful they became. Peepers and Squeakers got so they could glide over the ice and come in for a smooth landing that would have made a 747 pilot proud.

By the first week of January, their patch of open water was about twelve feet across. Sometimes fifty to seventy wild ducks would join them, helping with the shift work. They also enjoyed the leftovers of corn, wheat and oats. On January 17 the ice froze solid. The ducks stood on the ice so forlornly. "What do we do now?" they seemed to be saying.

I had to get on a ladder and get all the chicken wire, heat lamp, waterers and lumber we had carefully stored (thinking we would not need it) on the rafters of our garage. It was 24 degrees with the wind blowing outside. I am not a carpenter. But I rebuilt the duck house and made the wire cage big enough for the nineteen ducks to have walking space. I won't tell you the number of trips between the house and the lake, nor will I tell how many times the hammer made contact with my thumb. But in six hours I had it done.

Then I caught the ducks and put them all in the pen. They didn't even seem to appreciate all the trouble I had gone to just so they could be warm. I kept them there for four weeks, feeding them three times a day. They had lost at least half their body weight by the time the ice had frozen solid. So they needed the three feedings. The first week of February, it warmed up. I opened one end of the pen and let them out. They went straight to the lake. They went crazy. They splashed. They swam. They flapped their wings and dove in the water. They now stay as far away from that pen as possible.

They aren't too friendly with me either. After all that loving care I gave them! Just wait until they have ducks of their own someday!

# CHAPTER 12

# The Ducks Are Growing Up

Spring update. True love has come to the duck pond. It is a sight to behold. Remember those dear, loving ducks that have been a tight, cohesive group since they were one day old? The ducks that ate together, slept together, swam together, waddled up to the house together?

No more. When the grass started turning green, their hormones went into action. The males turned into egotistical self-centered sheiks. They preen and strut. Their necks go up and down saying, "Look at me, you lucky ducky ladies." I cannot translate their quacking and cooing, but I think they are singing, "Swimming on the corner watching the girls go by."

To be fair, I need to add that the females are playing their role to the hilt too. I am glad I kept the numbers of males and females equal. Otherwise I would be looking in the yellow pages for a duck psychologist about now. No longer do I have a group of ducks. It is every mallard for himself. I don't think they believe in women's lib. The female caters to her mate. She swims at his side, two strokes behind him. He comes to dinner in the lead. She follows. When he heads back to the lake, she trails behind.

And the fighting! One duck has a patch of feathers missing from his back. Evidently he was thinking of flirting when given a come-hither look of a hen. Each pair has a certain territory. When a debonair male or a flirtatious female tries a little dalliance, the fight is on. The dumb ducks do not understand that if each male picks one female and they remain committed to each other that they can live happily ever after—or at least until their hormones calm down. But no, one male has two girlfriends. So this throws the balance off. Therefore, there is always one lonesome male on the prowl. (Or should I say on the stroke?) He follows first one couple, and then another, looking for female companionship. If he does win the female over, then the jilted duck has to look for a new conquest.

Sounds a lot like the goings-on in a high school, doesn't it? They all got along fine until the love bug bit. They used to come in a rush when I would call. Now it takes ten minutes for them to decide who is going to walk by whom, and if one male gets too close to another's mate, the call to supper is forgotten.

The females must know some of the current trends in society, however. None of them seem in any hurry to settle down and raise a family. One neighbor told me he saw duck eggs abandoned along the edge of the lake. Someone else reported seeing four eggs under two feet of water. Don't you think they would settle down and leave the running-around scene at this stage in their lives? That they would opt instead for the trusted love and commitment of one mate? Maybe I did not make the rewards of parenting clear enough. I am going to try to make amends. I got that book *Joy of Parenting*. I will read it to them this afternoon. It is either that or demonstrate sitting on an egg—and I draw the line there.

A family who lived in Colstrip has had four mallard ducks for over a year. They raised them from babies. The ducks lived in their backyard and did tricks like diving off a ledge into the pool. Two weeks ago the family called and asked if I would consider adopting their ducks since the backyard just seemed too confining for the full-grown ducks. The family thought the ducks would enjoy the lake behind our house.

"I would be glad to take the ducks," I said. So on Sunday night they brought the four ducks and a supply of food to our house. The parting with their ducks was a little emotional. I am glad I am not the only one who is silly about this duck business. We took the ducks down to the lake. The family went home. My ducks swam around, checking out the new arrivals—especially the females since we are still in that season! The new ducks seemed to adapt well.

However, two days later I got a call from my neighbor at the end of our street. "Lois, four of your ducks are walking down the street. They are headed south."

"Thanks much," I said. Leaping into the car, I started my search. I figured which four ducks these were. I was right. They were my new "adopted" children-ducks, and they were headed home. I could just hear them saying, "Thank you very much, the vacation at your resort was nice. Now we'll be on our way." With the help of two friends and lots of effort, we caught the four wanderers. I put the ducks in a box in the car, covered them with a blanket and took them back home.

I put them in my duck pen. I decided they needed to get accustomed to the new surroundings. I watered and fed them three times a day. I fed my ducks right beside the pen so they could all get acquainted. We kept them penned up for four days. Then I went on a trip to Wyoming. I asked Robert to let them out on Saturday. He did. And in just a few hours the phone rang.

"There are four ducks walking down the street. The dogs are following their parade closely. They are almost downtown." Ross was the only one home and even though he likes the ducks he didn't think duck-sitting was one of his chores! So he called the "parents" of the four ducks. With the help of their daughter, he managed to round up the wandering foursome again. This time the heartstrings tugged and the family gave in. They picked up their duck food and refilled their wading pool. After all, sometimes these kids just aren't ready to leave home.

### BIRTH ANNOUNCEMENT

Announcing . . . four baby ducks
Weight . . . 6 ounces
Birthdate . . . June 2
Coloring . . . brown and yellow fuzzy
Parents . . . Daisy and Festus Duck

Yes, we have baby ducks! I never thought it would happen. I had given up on parenthood for my ducks. I would never be a duck-grandma. All spring, they laid eggs everywhere. Wherever I walked along the lake, I would see abandoned duck eggs. They even laid them in the water. None of the hens seemed interested in nest-sitting. I had seen broken eggs and abandoned nests. Every apparent marriage was soon broken as one of the couple would choose another mate. My ducks really seem to be a fickle bunch.

Thursday night we heard some peeping . . . and soon discovered the four tiny fuzzy babies. Mama Duck was nervously quacking, urging her young ones to stay close. She didn't even let me, Grandma, get close enough to take pictures. She keeps them hidden in the cattails around the edge of our cove. She isn't interested in showing them off to the other ducks, either. She wants no company around her little brood. They must be eating well, because they have doubled in size in three days.

These ducks have really been a learning experience for me. Now I have a new set of problems. Like what do you get a baby duck? And who do I invite to a baby shower? And should I serve cake—or duck food?

These ducks have really been a learning experience for me. Now I have a new set of problems. Like what do you get a baby duck? And who do I invite to a baby shower? And should I serve cake—or duck food?

The Forsyth Area Chamber of Commerce has set July 30 as the date of the first annual Yellowstone River Duck Festival. You can bet I am going to participate. I have already purchased my yellow rubber duck for the Rubber Duck Race at 4 p.m. on Saturday. I wanted to buy more than one but Robert said no. I think he is still regretting saying "yes" a year ago to the twenty-two live baby ducks I brought home.

The Duck Festival is a fund-raising event. You can buy a rubber duck for $10 from any Chamber of Commerce member. The ducks will be tossed (gently, I hope) into the Yellowstone River west of Forsyth. The first duck to cross the finish line one mile down the river at the bridge will win $1,000 for its owner. That is incentive enough for me. Almost incentive enough to really get desperate about this.

Gil Fennern, a Chamber member, told me one scheme had already been uncovered. The unscrupulous duck owner was going to pound several Alka-Seltzers into a fine powder and sift it into the duck's squeaker. There was an engineering problem in getting the "propellant" aimed, however. Someone suggested I could paint one of my own ducks yellow and let it swim to the finish line. I am afraid I would get caught at that. Besides, God watches over me. So would the judges who are checking each duck at the entry gate.

So I have decided on a much more humane, honest method. I am coaching my yellow rubber duck. He is now in official training. I am using the positive-thinking approach. I set him on the table while I have my morning coffee. I say, "Duck #133, you are going to win that race." Every few minutes I repeat the phrase. Then when I go to my desk to work I take Duck with me. "You are a fast duck," I tell him. "I have never known a faster duck." At night, I set him beside the bed, again repeating positive statements. I was thinking of buying one of those positive thinking subliminal tapes, but Robert said that was going a little too far.

One thing I have to check on before the day of the race concerns the retrieval plan. I certainly hope the Chamber members have thought about this. Whether Duck #133 wins or not, I still want him back. We have developed quite a relationship these last few days. I am sure the other duck owners feel the same. I cannot imagine that they are going to abandon the losers. I would be awake all night worrying about those helpless little rubber ducks floating down to the Mississippi.

I sure would like to win that $1,000. It would balance the deficit in our family budget under Duck Expense. This positive thinking approach has got to work. I tried dipping one of my ducks into a bucket of yellow food coloring and it didn't work at all. You could tell right away he was a live duck—he didn't have a squeaker.

Note: I really didn't try to dye a duck. I really didn't win the $1,000 either. By the way, for those of you on the great Mississippi, if you see a yellow rubber duck floating by, would you check and see if he has #133 tattooed on his bottom?

Sometimes I think I would be better off if I were just quiet more often! I was praying with a friend this week and giggled when I heard a statement of her prayer. It made sense when you heard what she said before and after, but I just caught one phrase, "Lord, shut my mouth before I take another step," she prayed earnestly. I don't think the Lord would have minded my giggle. He may have smiled too.

The Bible says the tongue is difficult to tame. Sometimes I think my tongue runs faster than my brain. If I would stop and think before speaking, I wouldn't get my foot in my mouth so often. Maybe I should pray that same prayer.

Other people say things with double meanings. I laughed at the comment from a friend at church camp this year, "I am so sorry to hear you lost your voice." Hmmm.

My dad gives instructions to my mom when they are loading the horses at the ranch or loading cattle in the stock truck. Many are the times I have heard him tell my mom, "Go ahead and back up." It is a good thing they have been married and working together for so many years. She knows what he means is "OK, you can back up now."

I was visiting Roy Edwards. He raises ducks too. I was happy to learn that one of his hens had successfully sat on her eggs and hatched three baby ducklings. I was anxious to learn how they were doing. He said, "Well, they did pretty good at first. Stayed right around the house and swam in the pond. But one morning I went out and two of them showed up missing."

I guess David must have had the same trouble that some of us do. In Psalm 141:3, he prays, "Set a guard over my mouth, O LORD; keep watch over the door of my lips." I can say "Amen" to that.

"Lois, this is Sandy," the caller said. "Congratulations, you are grandma!"

"Of what?"

"I just saw a lady drive down by the lake," she said. "She and her boys got out of their car, ran down to the lake, threw in some ducks and left."

"They didn't just happen to leave a bag of food, did they?"

She laughed, "Dream on!" She and John had raised ducks and geese. They knew about the feed bills. Sure enough, the next day my flock had grown from twenty-six to twenty-eight. I started this summer with nineteen ducks. You remember the trauma I went through to give twenty ducks away a year ago.

So for a little arithmetic problem: Lois had nineteen ducks. The ducks had sixteen babies. Only one baby duck survived thanks to northern pike, foxes, coyotes, skunks and poor mothering skills! Lois did not buy any more ducks. Now she has twenty-eight. How many ducks were donated to Lois?

You know about Peepers and Squeakers. They came last year and are part of the nineteen. Their former owners visit them and bring food for them. Another family asked us to take four ducks but the ducks did not want to stay. Six ducks were brought by a family who called and checked with us first. I have thought of applying for a government grant. I could open a foster care center for ducks. People are really concerned about the homeless. I would be a shelter for abandoned ducks. A Duck Rescue Mission.

So here is the second problem: what is Lois going to do with the extra ducks who won't fit in her duck house? It holds twenty. If you have a solution, let me know. And don't mention Thanksgiving dinner, either. First prize is eight ducks delivered to your door.

Winter report, second year. If you want to use the expression "like a duck takes to water," be sure that you are using it appropriately. I can tell you how a duck takes to water: joyously, gaily, gleefully, freely and full of life. It is a celebration. I know this is true. When the ice on the lake melted this spring, my twenty-eight ducks discovered the open water and went nuts splashing and diving. If it hadn't been for the quacking, you would have thought it was a sheepherder indulging in his spring bath.

This was a bad winter for the ducks. I tried to keep a hole in the ice open for them. It kept shrinking. The ice got thicker. I used an oar, a board, the hoe and an ax in my efforts to break the ice. After I broke a hockey stick (well, it was hanging in the garage and seemed like a good idea) and my husband's shovel handle, I gave up.

From January to the end of March the ducks had to sit huddled on the edge of the ice. They would not go in Duck Haven. It was too small. I took water to them every day and feed. I took straw bales down for shelter. At first they would sit around the outside of the straw bales and shiver. I gave them a lecture about being too dumb for their own good. Then they moved into the straw. The temperatures dipped to 28 below that day so maybe it wasn't my lecture after all. I fed twenty to forty wild ducks through the winter also. They had discovered the free soup line for the homeless and needy (duck variety).

They all survived. I did not lose a duck. Now they are in the prom season. True love and mating are preceded by chasing, fighting and flirting. Pairs are established. The pack of ducks is again nonexistent. They are private and standoffish. Soon they will be laying eggs. I hope this year they are better parents. The one baby duckling who survived last year we named Jonah. Jonah is a neat duck because he is a cross between a mallard and a white duck. Jonah is a fitting name for one who survived. Only now I have a problem. Jonah got a spring coat of new feathers and he is a she. Joannah?

It looks like Spring is walking back into Montana. Carpets of green grass and blooming daffodils herald her arrival. And she brings a basket of work over her arm. Farmers on tractors and gardeners with shovels are turning the soil. I was in Wyoming last week for speaking engagements. Everywhere I drove there were new calves, lambs and colts. Our baby ducks are following their moms down at the lake.

Branding, planting, irrigating, mowing and weeding will soon take all of the time of my folks and the ranchers and farmers around us.

Of course we love the arrival of Spring. She is the promise of new life. So we accept the first sunburn, long hours with the tractor or hoe and sore muscles with the anticipation that our work will bear fruit.

Now let me make a comparison. How is your marriage doing? Is it in need of new life? Are you and your spouse growing closer together or more distant? Ray Ortlund, pastor and radio host said, "Marriage is like a plant. It is either growing or dying." As we walk through life's daily routines, we can begin to take our marriage partners for granted. We don't give a lot of attention or time to daily marriage care.

I can guarantee you that if you leave that garden to fend for itself after you plant it, you are not going to have much "fruit." There will be weeds, bugs and lots of dead plants instead of a harvest. You can blame the weather. Too much sun. Not enough rain. You can blame the neighbors. Their weeds blew your way. There are lots of excuses. The true reason for dying plants is lack of care. Care is nurturing. Care is feeding and watering. Care is spending time and energy on the plants. Care is protecting them from storms by being ready for them.

It is the same in our marriages. Many times we get so busy with our work and schedules that our marriage partners get less "care" than all our other responsibilities. Marriage care involves spending time with each other alone. It means really listening to each other. It means praying together. Going places together. Little gifts and notes say, "I love you enough to take the time to do extra special things for you."

For us to say, "I love you," and then never exert energy toward improving and building the relationship is like talking about how much we love to garden—and never lifting a hoe. And just like our gardens, the time and attention spent on our marriages will increase the harvest—the fruit. Do you want new life in your marriage? Roll up your sleeves, put on your gloves and get to work! Happy spring! The season of promise of good things to come!

Fall report. Next in the saga of the ducks. I started the year with twenty-two ducks. Now I have forty. That is forty ducks to care for and feed. My trips to Forsyth Seed and Feed are becoming more frequent. My dad gave me a couple of bags of grain, which certainly helped. But I am getting a little concerned.

Winter will be here soon. Winter with ducks means chopping holes in the ice, building shelter and getting bedding straw. When I can no longer chop through the ice, I carry water three times a day.

Last year when I broke Robert's shovel handle and then a hockey stick trying to break through the ice in the lake, I gave up. Then for five weeks I had to haul water. I know whose idea it was to get ducks in the first place. Mine. But the increase in population is not all my fault. People keep dropping ducks off. Last week six new ducks appeared. One was black with a tuft of hair on his head and a broken beak. Now I am running a duck orphanage.

My ducks learned the principles of hatching better this year. Last year one duckling survived. This year I am grandmother to seventeen. There were actually twenty-six born. At least the odds have improved this year.

So now Lois has forty ducks. That is a lot of ducks. I would be glad to give you one or two. Of course I have to keep Peepers and Squeakers. And Jonah and Festus and Hezekiah and Wimpy and Harry. There should still be enough to go around. Call me if you would like a duck. Robert says he will even deliver them.

January 11: Peepers and Squeakers, the two white ducks are gone. Hezekiah is gone. Festus is gone. Jonah and her baby are gone. All of the ducks are gone except one.

On December 23 I had eighteen ducks when they came to eat their supper. (My friend had again come to my rescue in the fall to take twenty-two ducks to his place. I was nice to him this time.) I was so glad they had all survived the 30-below weather of the week before. People kept telling me I shouldn't be worried. "Ducks are covered with down," I was told. "You don't have to worry about them."

I guess they were right because they all looked fine that evening. Robert went down to feed them Christmas Eve. When he came back to the house he said, "Six of your ducks didn't show up."

"They must not have been hungry," I said. Rarely did the ducks not come when we called. But now and then it had happened.

"Only one white duck came," he said. Now that was strange because Peepers and Squeakers have always been first in line for food. When people came to feed them the white ducks were always the first to eat out of the strangers' hands. They weren't afraid of kids, either. And they always stayed together.

Christmas morning I looked out on the ice-covered lake as soon as it was light. I could see the ducks all huddled together.

"I'll go down and feed the ducks," Robert told me right after we opened our presents.

*He's worried too,* I thought to myself.

"Now both Peepers and Squeakers are gone," he reported as he took off his coat.

"They are both gone?"

"Yes and four more."

"Four more?" I said. It just was not making sense.

"You have seven ducks left."

It wasn't long before I knew I wasn't the only one in this family attached to our feathered pets. "I'll go down and look around," said Ross, who was home from college. We watched from the window. When he got near the tiny flock of ducks that were left, they lit out across the lake running and flying. That added to the mystery because they hadn't done that since this fall when I gave the extra ducks away.

Later in the day Robert came into the kitchen where I was preparing Christmas dinner. "I just walked the four miles all around the lake. I can't see any of them." I told him I had done the same thing earlier while he was downstairs.

He read my mind. "I can't see any feathers or blood or sign of a struggle. They have just disappeared."

The next day I started asking around the neighborhood. Everyone had seen or heard coyotes this fall but no one had seen any signs of them around the ducks. People tried to reassure me, "Maybe they just flew away." I knew that didn't happen because I have had these ducks for three and a half years. They did everything as a group. If one had flown, they would have all gone. They never did learn to fly well anyway.

The next day when we went down with their supper, I couldn't keep the tears back. One mallard came quacking across the ice toward us. By himself. All alone. Whatever mysterious duck-napping sleuth that lurked in the dark of night had returned. Here was the lone survivor.

As close as I have been to these ducks (some since they were twenty-four hours old) I could not communicate with him so I could learn what happened. We put him in the pen so he wouldn't disappear and gave him straw, oats and water. "We should have had them all in the pen," I wailed. "We should have . . ."

"Lois, don't do that. They were doing just fine. You couldn't have known this would happen. Animals in the wild are vulnerable."

"I should have just penned them up. Why didn't I pen the last seven up?"

"Because you were just believing the episode was over." Robert was holding me. Tears flooded the front of his warm red winter coat. After a while we walked back up to the house.

I do not know what happened. We have driven all over Colstrip and the surrounding area where there are open bodies of water. There are lots of ducks—but none of mine. We have asked everyone from ice fishermen on the lake to all the neighbors who cared about the ducks. No one has seen anything out of the ordinary.

This isn't the way I wanted "The Saga of the Ducks" to end. And it isn't the way the brave duck huddled all by himself down in the pen at the edge of our lawn wanted it either. I am sad and I think he is sad too.

However, I am thanking the Lord for the stories and lessons from the ducks since I have had them . . . the way the kids' faces lit up when they fed them . . . the way they quacked when I called . . . the way they followed us in our canoe on the lake . . .

Just don't anybody say to me, "Oh, honestly, Lois, they were just ducks." I know that—and right now I am missing my friends—who were just ducks!

# CHAPTER 13

# Travelin'

G od made men and women different. He must have, because men just think differently than women do. They do things differently too. First, let me say that I am not men-bashing. It's just that vacation time is approaching. I thought I should write about some of the hazards of traveling with your spouse. And I love my spouse.

But . . . when we travel, we have a few "diffugalities." Our trip to Florida in December was no exception. We had a beautiful flight. But the minute we landed in Tampa, I knew it would happen again, just like it had in Los Angeles, Dallas, San Diego and Baton Rouge. We present our papers for a rental car—that he reserved—and load our bags into the car. He gets behind the wheel of whatever new snappy model he has dreamed about driving for weeks and puts it in gear. We immediately head out of the commotion-filled car lot into the bumper-to-bumper four-lane traffic of a busy airport. He sees a car length of open space in the race of hundreds of cars driving over the speed limit and zips us up into the line of traffic.

I hang on to the console and my door handle while overhead exit signs list fourteen options. I diligently try to read each one as designated trip-navigator with the highlighted Avis map on my lap.

But the driver, is he reading the signs? *No.* He is trying the automatic rearview mirror buttons on the door armrest. From there he moves to the air conditioner. We are snapped with high cool, low fan, medium temperature, maximum breeze and open vent as he pushes buttons. He moves from there to the steering wheel. The wheel tilts from the dash to his lap as six positions are tested. All while we are the merg-er and merg-ee in the race for the airport exit. If I have yelled "Now!" at the appropriate time, we maneuver onto the packed freeway.

"Today in Tampa we have overcast skies and later we can expect . . . be-bop-a-do, oh, how I love . . . then if you have termites you can call . . . friends in low places . . . in Washington D.C. the President said . . . my achy breaky heart . . . " He is trying out the radio! The station digits race as fast as the 6 million cars behind us.

Just as I think he has tried every button, the seat moves. Up, down, back. The headrest tilts. The windows whoosh down as the automatic door lock by my shoulder clicks shut. Just as I am trying to find a street sign that matches one on the sweaty map in my lap, the dome light comes on and the visor is down.

"Look at this, hon," he says, "a lighted mirror! Great, huh?"

Now, you see, if I were driving this car, we'd still be at the airport in the rental lot. I'd have to be checking out our route, adjusting the mirrors and fastening my seat belt. With him, we are already on our way . . . where, I am not exactly sure. I cannot read the map when I am terrified out of my mind.

So now we could be lost. No, I mean *I* could be lost. Men never get lost. But that's another story.

I love you, Robert!

No matter where you live in Montana, the fourth largest state in the United States, you are used to lots of miles on the road. While there are three or four major centers of population in the state in cities, most of our state could be classified as rural population. We have lots of small towns in our fifty-six counties. And many of our routine needs, whether medical, agricultural, major airports recreation or business needs, necessitate a trip of several hours. We are thankful for those hardy small town businesses that do allow us to get most basic needs and emergency medical care in our respective communities.

Robert and I were coming back one Saturday evening after a day in Billings, 130 miles away. He had worked on the car of our college son, Ross. I, being a typical mom, had cleaned his apartment and replenished his cupboards. We were both tired and both quiet on the trip home.

An hour and the miles slipped by. He'd take a sip of his iced tea in his insulated mug every now and then and I finished off my mug filled with coffee. As usual my mind had already thought through a hundred different subjects, from kids, to work, to writing ideas, to jobs I need to get done, to budget matters and even a few national issues (which, of course, I had the answers to if anyone cared to ask me).

I glanced at Robert. "What do you think about life?" I asked. He had one hand on the steering wheel and was taking a swallow of tea. We had just passed the Hysham exit on I-94.

"What?"

"I said, 'What do you think about life?' " I repeated.

"What kind of question is that?"

We have been married a long time. I know we are different. We can be driving down the road with a long period of silence and I'll say, "What are you thinking?" and he'll say, "About what?" And I'll say, "About anything. What are you thinking about right now?" and he'll answer, "Nothing. I'm just driving."

That boggles my mind. When driving, I pray, I sing. I listen to tapes. I solve family matters. I solve world situations. I even solve stuff that is none of my business. And he says he is driving along, just driving! I am sure a patrolman would consider his driving safer than mine. But look at all the world problems I am finding solutions to!

We were about to turn off the interstate onto Highway 39 when he said, "I still haven't answered your question, have I?"

"Nope," I said. It was killing me but I had determined to keep my mouth shut until he gave me an answer. I didn't want to be tricked into casual conversation.

"Well . . . here is what I think . . ." he started, and soon we were immersed in a conversation of life, our future, highlights of the past years, what meant the most to us during our life together, and of course how his dream of owning a junkyard (called Sanford and Lois) was still in his mind. I didn't tell him that the whole time I was quiet I really wasn't. I was praying that God would make this time special for us. And He did. We were still sharing thoughts as we unloaded our purchases of the day from the car and walked in our house. Oh, how I love that man—and my Lord who hears my prayers on little things too.

It reminded me of a comment I heard Sharon Burton make one time. We were visiting with some newcomers to Colstrip. We had asked how they were adjusting. One lady said, "We really like the town and the people. It's just so far to anywhere."

Sharon replied, "That's the best part of living here. The time our family or my husband and I spend driving places is precious. We have one or two or four hours to spend together. No phones. No interruptions. I wouldn't trade those times for anything!"

I agreed with Sharon wholeheartedly, although now a lot of us have cell phones to keep in touch when we're out on the road. We Montanans are blessed with our travelin' hours. We get the magnificent scenery in Big Sky Country and we get quality time with our families (even if we have to get it moving with prayer sometimes). By the way, Sharon still doesn't have a cell phone. She refuses to get one. And I know why.

The reason we married folk sometimes have little discussions over driving goes back to my first comment in this chapter: men and women are different. They think differently. I can give you a perfect example: going to the city to shop with one's spouse.

We will need a map. I have provided one below even though I know that men do not need maps. The map:

Colstrip_____A____B_C_____D__Billings

At Point A we encounter our first problem.

*Point A.* "Well, what do ya want to do?" the man says. If the woman were driving, this question would not be asked. Because the woman knows (and has known for a week) what they need to buy (she has a list), where they need to go, which store has the best price, what aisle it is in and exactly how many seconds it will take for her to get it.

*Point B.* "Where do ya want to go first?" Second moot point. The woman has a schedule in her head. Some women will even have it numbered on their "Billings List." Any woman knows you start at either the east end or the west end and work your way through the list. Which brings us to:

*Point C.* No woman would ever go look at a part in the Heights on Billings' east end, then drive to K-Mart on the west end of Billings, then back up 24th Street, east to Grand Avenue to the Checker store for oil, then drive out the south exit to the truck stop for a cup of coffee, then back across Billings to Sears for a mower part. (OK, so I am exaggerating a little!)

*Point D.* "Let's stop and leave those glasses at the mall to get fixed. That way they will be done when we finish our shopping on the west end. That way we can have lunch at that new restaurant by the mall since it will be lunch time about then," she says. All of the woman's thinking is based on pure logic.

For a woman, a trip to Billings is not a play day (unless, of course, she has penciled that in on the calendar this month). It is a game of Concentration, MazeMasters, The Price Is Right, Jeopardy and Monopoly all rolled into one.

For a man, a trip to Billings is to be endured. Unless, of course, he doesn't take his spouse.

The elderly gentleman wore a blue Farmers Co-op cap and a blue jacket. He sat in the chair next to me in the crowded waiting room in the Billings Clinic. He and I went from "It sure looks like it could snow" to the possibilities of a hard winter in a few minutes.

From there we passed through Colstrip, where I live, to Joliet, where he lives. We covered the "Do you know who's." From there we went to bygone days. This was, I noticed, much to the relief—or boredom—of those around us.

"Yup, I am the longest taxpaying resident of Joliet. I live in the house my parents lived in," he told me. I got up for a cup of coffee and asked him if he wanted one.

"No, can't drink the stuff."

"Were you born there in Joliet?" I asked.

"No, I came there after the Depression. There weren't many jobs during the Depression, you know. I was from back East. A friend and I hopped a freight and went looking for work. Most of the states . . . they were pretty good to guys riding on the rails. Not in Washington, though . . . they'd kick you right off. Even take a stick to you!"

I wasn't the only one interested in this bit of history being told in the waiting room. "How did you find work?" I asked.

"Well, we traveled all over the country finding work here and there for a few weeks. One time we were in Indiana. We paid a guy named Wally $2.50 to find us a job. The job was supposed to last four days but it only lasted two days. We were paid $4. We went back to Wally and raised a ruckus. He told us that that job usually took four days but since we were such hard workers we had done it in half the time," he laughed.

"I bet $2.50 was a lot of money in those days," I said.

"It was. But Wally came through for us. He put us on a rail job. That lasted a week. Then the foreman came around with our pay and pink slips. I told him I needed to keep working. So he sez to me, 'Go down to the other end of the rail, I'll talk to you later.'" My newfound friend smiled. "And I worked for the railroad for forty more years!"

"Lois Olmstead?" The nurse had my chart in her hand.

"Good chatting with you," I said as I jumped up. "Wish we could talk more," I said, shaking his hand. "Hope your tests come out good. God bless!"

I think God allows delays. I know He does. I have read about them in my Bible. The significance of such delays in the Bible lies in the reasons for the holdups. God always had a lesson or purpose in what seemed to an individual to be an annoying delay.

I could get procrastination awards in stuff like cleaning, paying bills and balancing checkbooks. But in the other areas of my life I am overly punctual. Delays in schedules give me fits!

However, I am trying to learn patience. I am practicing these words: *God allows delays*! I may not understand or like it. Just possibly it could be "allowed" for my benefit. Delays. Waiting.

The secret to delay-mastery lies first in trusting God, then being on the lookout for serendipity-possibilities (SPs). If you aren't familiar with them, look in your dictionary. Or just remember my friend in the blue Farmer's Co-op cap. Our conversation was a SP to the max!

And I didn't know it then, but I was going to find out much about trips to Billings and the Billings Clinic. A big change occurred in our lives on January 31, 1992. This trip would be 8,850 miles. I wrote a column about it:

"Zlang!" I heard the sound of metal hitting metal. Robert was cutting his cinnamon roll in half so he could butter it.

"Drats! It must be the lid to the frosting can" I said.

"Oh," he said.

The man is a saint, you know. Some people would get really riled up finding a lid baked in their breakfast. Not Robert. Of course, he's used to that kind of thing.

It was Sunday, a beautiful day when I pulled open the drapes. *We'll have a good home-cooked breakfast,* I thought. I had the perfect thing: pop-out-of-the-can cinnamon rolls with frosting. I put them in a baking dish. I did notice the frosting didn't have its little lid on it, but I ignored the fact. Then I raced on to do the part I like, before Robert got out of the shower. I set the table with pretty dishes, napkins and some flowers. It was perfect, too—until the "Zlang." But we had a good laugh, and knowing Robert, I will hear the story over more than once! I had been to the doctor on Friday for my yearly checkup and the mammogram revealed what appeared to be a malignant mass. I was scheduled for surgery on Monday.

So I could have said, "Oh, my mind was all shook up, so I wasn't paying attention to my cooking."

But that wasn't true for two reasons. First of all, I do this kind of thing all the time when I am cooking. Secondly, I wasn't all shook up. I don't say that with a proud or superhuman attitude—I just believe in God. He has taught me through the years that I can trust Him.

Through trials, teachings, Bible studies, sermons and sharing with other believers, I have learned that the Bible is true and God is all-sufficient when we put our trust in Him. He has been faithful through thirty years of marriage, raising three boys, through all my life. Through good experiences and not so good experiences. Through cooking experiences, making a wedding dress, speaking engagements and everything else. He was faithful to my parents and grandparents before.

Monday I went for the biopsy and surgery to remove the tumor and surrounding tissue and the lymph nodes from my left side. I came home on Wednesday. After Robert and I prayed and discussed the consultations with the doctors, my protocol (treatment) was decided. I began chemotherapy and radiation treatments a few weeks later.

So, dear faithful column readers, I am going to take time out from "Time Out With Lois" for a little while. When I write this column, I write about what is going on in my life. The next few months it is going to be medical and I doubt you'd want to read about that. I also had to cancel several speaking engagements and other commitments so as to give full time to following doctors' orders. I am going to switch into a listening mode for a while!

You know, that "Zlang" and discovery of that lid baked into Robert's breakfast roll didn't ruin that breakfast for us that Sunday. I don't want to compare an encounter with cancer with my cooking follies—yet I do. I trust God for my every day and for these days that lie ahead. (Robert puts his life in my hands every time I enter the kitchen!)

I know God is sufficient for all of my needs. My soul mate, our children, parents and friends have overwhelmed me with their love and prayers. Please continue to pray for them because it is hard for them. I have lots and lots of Bible verses I love, but read Proverbs 3:5 and 6 and Isaiah chapter 43.

Thanks for all your kindnesses to our family. You all are a blessing to us.

And that column began the steps into an eventful year. My experience with cancer has been chronicled in the book *Breast Cancer and Me,* published by Christian Publications. I hope you can read that book to understand how that year went for our family. One of the best ideas I had during that time involved my trips to Billings to the Northern Rockies Cancer Center for six weeks of radiation treatments.

"I think God just gave me an idea," I said to Robert as we were driving home from my appointment with Dr. Dennistoun Brown, my surgeon, a week after my surgery. "What if I had a different person drive me to Billings every day for radiation?"

"I want to drive you as much as I can," he said.

"Oh, I know. But you can't do it every day. I just think it would make the trip less boring if I had a different person driving me. Besides, it would be a test to see if I really have thirty-five friends!"

"Would you ride in their cars?"

"No, they could drive our car. I would just be the passenger. I can rest while they drive."

"Well, it might be a good idea. Would you only want people from church?"

"No," I was getting excited now with the whole idea. "I could just put the word out and see who volunteers. And there would be rules too."

"Rules?"

"Yup, rules. First, no one could have two turns, except for you, of course." I reached over and patted his shoulder.

"What're the other rules?"

"Well, I don't want anyone that drives really slow—that would drive me nuts! And those are the only two rules I can think of right now."

"We don't even know if you're going to be driving every day. What if you get sick?" Robert asked. "What if you decided to stay in Billings? What if the roads get bad?"

"Well, then we could just change the rules!"

The idea was great. I settled back in my seat thinking about the trips ahead of me. Dr. Lamm said I would need thirty to thirty-five radiation treatments. Robert will probably drive me at least five times. That means I need about thirty drivers . . .

And the idea was marvelous and worked out so well! (Get the book!) When we totaled up the trips, it was over 8,000 miles. We definitely had been traveling! We also learned we were right all along about the blessings of living in Colstrip, Montana!

# CHAPTER 14

# Colstrip

We first heard about the Colstrip project in 1970. The town was near the vast coal resources in southeastern Montana. The Northern Pacific Railroad had built the town in 1923 and mined the coal to use in their coal-fired locomotives. When diesel locomotives came, there was no longer a need for them to mine the coal. So for many years the mine was idle. Colstrip, with thirty-eight houses, a school and around 200 people, survived. In 1958, the Montana Power Company bought the town (it had been owned by Northern Pacific), the mine and equipment. It was in 1970 that the utility company decided to build electrical generation facilities on the site.

The population of Colstrip exploded to over 8,000 during construction. Creative planning went into a master plan to make the expansion a beautiful and comfortable community with new schools and recreation and business opportunities. The population after the construction of the four generating plants settled in around 3,500. It was remarkable to be involved with the rebirth of a community. We prayed, asking God to let us go and be a part of this adventure. God said, "Yes!"

*December 27, 1973, 6:00 p.m.* The address is 241 Fair Park Drive, Billings, and I am sitting on the freshly cleaned carpet in an empty house. The spell is broken by the men in my family, husband Robert, and three boys, ages eleven, eight and five, yelling, "Come on, Mom!

173

At last we are on our way to our new home in Colstrip. Hurry up!" And so we are on our way—in the midst of one of those December blowing snowstorms.

Our caravan heads east. Our family possessions, including those just-unwrapped, then packed-up Christmas presents, led the procession in a long orange moving van. "I wish those movers would have hurried more with their loading. We should have been on our way hours before now," I say to myself. I follow the moving van in our car with a tall green leafy begonia, our dog, Muffin, a laundry basket of freshly dried clothes I snatched out of the dryer as it was being loaded onto the van—and our two youngest boys, Kevin and Ross. Todd is riding with his dad in the pickup behind us. They are loaded with all the things the movers cannot take—paint, varnish, spray cans and the garden hose.

It only takes thirty miles of driving in the eerie world of headlights and blinding snowflakes on the narrow two-lane road (now four-lane Interstate 94) to make me wish we had never heard of Colstrip. Every time I meet a big truck I am blinded by the snow, and letting up on the gas causes the car to slip sideways. Every few minutes, one of the boys asks, "Are we about to Colstrip?" I can see the headlights of our pickup behind us.

Later, Kevin reported, "Mom just said, 'Here we go' and there we went!" Praise the Lord that there was no oncoming traffic as the car suddenly slipped on the ice, went skating across the road and swayed teetering on the edge of the highway before deciding not to tip over but slide down the embankment and come to rest with the two front wheels over a ditch bank.

The interior of the car was a mess. Muffin was trapped under the laundry basket, barking, the begonia was leaning precariously over my shoulder, clothes were everywhere and the two boys were crying, "We want Daddy. We want to ride with Daddy!"

And me: I had planned carefully for my entrance into Colstrip. As sensible as always, I had worn my new knee-length fur-cuffed coat and fashion boots with two-inch heels. Because there was not time during the move for a trip to the beauty shop, I had donned my then-in-fashion elegantly styled wig—which was now off my head and hanging over my ear with a single bobby pin! I did the first thing any sensible, loving wife would do in such a desperate situation. I pushed open the car door and fell into eighteen inches of snow. *"Robert! Help!"* I yelled.

He came, terrified as he had watched the entire scene. Someone went for help, then the highway patrol and the wrecker came. Soon the car was back on the road, where I straightened my wig with determination and stated to Robert that I would drive on only as far as the next town. I was shaking like a leaf and it wasn't from the cold.

We spent that night in Custer, Montana in two separate motel rooms—not intentionally, but because the motel had no rooms with two beds. Somehow five of us, the dog and the begonia in one bed was not appealing. The next morning we continued our trip, bedraggled and wrinkled, to our new home. We moved into one of the newly constructed apartment buildings, not unpacking too much, because houses were being built as quickly as possible for new residents. And our Colstrip adventure had begun.

The one phone booth near the high school was kept busy. New phone lines could not be put in until spring when the ground thawed. Often there was a line of new residents waiting to call a wife, mother or both. We soon learned that to be happy at that time one had to believe that patience is a virtue. So much needed to be built in such a short time. Our house was done three months later so we finally unpacked those presents and had Christmas all over again.

My journal states that a typical day started with coffee at a neighbor's house. The day might include several gals in one car heading thirty-seven miles over chuckholes and a narrow road to Forsyth for groceries, gas and eating out. Or we might go eighty miles to Miles City for shopping, doctoring and eating out. On the weekends families would travel 130 miles west to Billings for shopping, a movie and eating out. Everyone lived with lists—grocery lists, catalog lists, Forsyth lists and Billings lists.

And there were parties, always with coffee and dessert: welcome-to-Colstrip parties, leaving-Colstrip parties, birthday parties (people moved to Colstrip with two vehicles, lots of kids and pets), Tupperware parties and Home Interior parties. I often worried that since we were living in similar houses, buying the same Tupperware and the same Home Interior décor for our walls—that our husbands working at the same jobs at the same plants might come home to the wrong house and not even know it!

Individuality did come, though. Many clubs and churches and groups were formed. We donned our work clothes, scraped paint, scrubbed floors, painted walls, begged for books and started the Colstrip Library. In a town with no shopping, no malls, no theaters or other conveniences, some folks were having a tough time adapting. We thought a library would help.

We could buy bread, eggs or milk at the Fountain, which was a gathering place for both new and old residents in the basement of the school that housed all twelve grades. I met Isabel Bills, for whom one of the new elementary schools is named, over a cup of coffee at the Fountain. Through her and some of her friends, we were able to start Friendship Bible Coffees which were a blessing to many construction wives and others in the community.

One of the pile of benefits that our family has received from living in "boomtown" was the friendships with a myriad of different folks. Isabel was one of the many who have made a lasting impression on my life. There was Narvell from Kentucky who taught me how to really scrub a floor. Joan, who taught the Catholic priest, Father Wally, how to open the parish oven door with a kick and a few words he had not heard before. Doc and Jean from Illinois with their eight children, to whom we showed the best camping spots, and Nick, a rancher and native of Rosebud County, who showed us how to cut off a rattlesnake head with a well-swung belt buckle. Ruth from New Zealand, and Mrs. Dibble, the town's only senior citizen and . . . we could go on and on.

We soon realized we were living in a fish bowl. It seemed that everyone from the local paper to the national television networks wanted to know all about life in Colstrip. Several of us were written about in a book by Mike Parfit called *Last Stand at Rosebud Creek*. It chronicled the struggles between the landowners and the utility companies. It soon became common to see a friend on TV or a neighbor's name in a national magazine. My journals and our scrapbooks are full of memories of those days of being modern-day pioneers.

Why did we pray to come to Colstrip? Because Robert was excited to be a part of the construction of these generation plants and seeing that energy being produced, and because we felt that it was where God was leading us.

Why do we love living in Colstrip? Because it never ceases to be an adventure. Throughout the years, we have met wonderful people, our children had excellent schools and the opportunities have been endless. Whether it is putting on an Easter pageant with all the churches involved, being a part of the mining or utility business or helping a family through a crisis, we still have a small-town atmosphere. Now, with some local stores supplying most of our needs and a new medical center, schools, a museum, parks and a golf course, we have seen lots of changes. Just this year, Colstrip became an incorporated city—with a real mayor. Now if we could just get a store that would sell underwear and socks, we'd have it made!

We have ended every Christmas letter since we were married with a verse from the Gospel of John: "Jesus said, 'I am come that you might have life, and that life, most abundant' " (John 10:10, author's para-phrase). Our Colstrip adventure is testimony to that.

Robert and I are thankful for God's answer of "Yes" to our Colstrip prayer.

# CHAPTER 15

## Life—
## An Adventure

I believe enough time has lapsed since this incident that I can tell it without fear of retribution (at least I hope so). I was elated when I heard Colstrip was getting a car wash. I had never used one before.

I had eight quarters and a dirty car. I drove the car into the stall and put four quarters in the machine. I turned the dial to Tire Wash and raced around the car spraying the tires with the high-pressure stream of water. Knowing time was of the essence, I turned the dial to Soapy Brush and prepared myself for a spray of suds—which didn't come. There was still just the stream of water—and not much water at that. I couldn't understand it. But the clock was ticking. I panicked. I feverishly went over the doors and fenders on one side with the trickle of water. Then the clock ran out. I put my last four quarters in the machine and left the dial at Soapy Brush hoping for the rush of sudsy water. Still only the small stream of water out of the nozzle at the end of the hosing gun. I was racing for time. I went over the hood and around the other side.

It was there I discovered the Soapy Brush! It was a separate brush with a separate hose, hanging on the opposite wall.

It was there I discovered the suds too! Lots of suds, suds a foot deep all over the floor of the carwash. I was wading in them!

I hurriedly glanced around for onlookers. The suds were making their way out of the car wash into the grocery store parking lot. At that moment, my second batch of quarters quit. The clock stopped and so did the water. I jumped in the car and headed for home, scared to death and feeling like a total idiot.

*At least no one needs to know,* I said to myself as I drove away. Then I looked in the rearview mirror. I was leaving a trail of white soapy suds behind me. It was not only that I was leaving a trail of guilt as I drove away—when I pulled into my driveway and got out of the car, I knew there would be plenty of evidence for the car wash police to convict me.

One side of the car looked like a zebra with clean stripes (where I had the trickle of water) interspersed with muddy stripes. The other side had little round dried bubbles of soap all along the side.

I then did the only thing I could do in light of the circumstances. I sat down and bawled.

My brother, Ron, with his wife, Sherri, make their home in western Wyoming where he works on a cattle ranch. Even though I think I got lots more spankings than he did growing up, he turned out OK after all. He is a real cowboy and an accomplished horseman.

Ron told me that when he first talked with the two rancher "businessmen," the conversation was not foreboding. As a matter of fact, it was flattering.

"We hear tell you are real good at breaking horses," they said. "We have a horse we'd like ya tah try. It's a four-year-old. Just halter broke." The lanky rancher was standing outside the rodeo arena where Ron had just finished his stint as rodeo judge. "We're willin' to pay ya for your trouble too." With a little hee-hawing, kicking dirt and corral fence-leaning, a deal was struck. They'd give Ron $450 a month. He'd break the horse to ride in a month or two. A handshake cemented the deal.

A week later the horse was delivered. Sherri always says you can tell a lot about a horse by looking at its eyes. Kind, gentle eyes mean a kind, gentle horse. That is what Sherri says. This horse had mean eyes. Downright wicked eyes. Ron should have paid more attention to Sherri's words right then.

Ron was up the next day at the crack of dawn as usual. He went down to the corral. First order of business was to hobble the horse. Then get a saddle on him. The second week Ron learned more about wicked-eyed horses. He had been kicked at and bulldozed by this horse the first week but he wasn't prepared for a direct charge attack.

They were in the barn alleyway. The horse charged. Ron ran. The horse chased him the length of the barn, right into the tack room, hobbles and all, wicked eyes flashing and mouth showing teeth. The teeth should have been a clue.

The next chapter unfolded out in the corral. Ron had the saddle on the horse. He tied a rope on the saddle horn. Then he bent down to wrap the rope around the front foot. The next part was quick. The horse bent down also and got a good bite of Ron's fleshy side above his belt. The horse says to himself, *When you're leading, keep leading! Pick 'em up high! Plunk 'em on the ground!* And he did. Ron was flat on his belly in the dirt, a horseshoe print on his backside.

With some iodine and bandages under his shirt, Ron was sore but determined. Three weeks later he was riding the horse around the corral. At five weeks into the venture the first $450 was definitely well earned and the horse was learning to submit to a rider. At least that is what Ron thought. "As a matter of fact, I was feelin' right confident . . . and lookin' forward to getting that check . . . and not just a little proud of my accomplishments with that darn horse," Ron told me. "He was shapin' out pretty good!" Then he told me the rest of the story.

"When I take a horse I am breakin' out of the corral, I run 'em up this hill behind the corrals to the top of a bluff. It takes the wind out of 'em. So that's what I did. I ran him out long and hard right to the top of the bluff. He was reining good. So I let him have a breather and wanted one myself. I just relaxed in the saddle . . . and the next thing I knew that horse took a leap. Right off the bluff. We were airborne. Then he slid right into an old dead tree. A dry branch pierced my leg on the way down. Tore my Levis!"

To Ron's credit, he was still in the saddle at the bottom. Blood was running down his leg and puddling in his boot as the horse continued his race straight to the corral. There, the horse stopped so abruptly the saddle horn drove into the crotch of the guy still in the saddle! But a cowboy with true grit never loses to a horse. A few more trips up the bluff (with no rest stops) and several longer rides and the horse was broke to ride. He called the rancher.

Ron had to lean against the corral fence when they came to pick up the horse. He just grunted when they asked why he was limping. They were very pleased with the horse. He took their check and said, "Nah, ain't got time," when they asked if he wanted to take on the three other four-year-olds they had.

When he called to tell me about this, he still had the check in his pocket. He'd been to the bank several times and the check wouldn't clear!

Dear Ron: I don't know why you are so worried about turning fifty on December 11. Any cowboy who can come through this tangle and still laugh has nothing to fear about getting old!

P.S. When Sherri says, "Look at the eyes!" I would if I wuz you! Love, your sis.

A trip to my folks' ranch yielded another husband-and-wife ranching tale. It seems Jim Taylor had a cow and her new calf in his round corral. The bonding that is supposed to take place naturally between mom-cow and baby-calf had not happened. Some human intervention was necessary.

This is usually accomplished by getting the pair together in a small space. The hunger of the newborn calf and the "cafeteria" equipment available on the cow normally respond with hands-on teaching in a small confined space. But mom-cow was on the fight this day on the Taylor ranch. Snorting snot and head down, she took after Jim the minute he got in the corral. He had a rope in hand and was determined to match this old gal with her new young-un'.

I need to explain that most ranchers have a "snubbing post" inside one of their corrals. This is a sturdy piece of equipment—either a big log post or a discarded railroad tie is used. Jim had the railroad tie. Big. Strong and sturdy and buried deep. All he had to do was rope mom-cow and dally the lariat around the snubbing post. ESPN should have had their cameras on the sports action in that corral. Not only were Jim's unsuccessful attempts at roping the old gal a show, but the speed of his trips made in the corral's soft dirt would have garnered him a world track record. Of course, the speed of his laps and the size of the cowhide-in-fury may have disqualified him. The lined, suntanned face of the young rancher broke into a self-effacing grin when he summed up the event for me.

"That snubbing post was the size of a toothpick before I gave up and jumped the fence!"

Mom-cow didn't win. Jim marched straight to the house and yelled to his wife (don't they always?), "Roxy, get the pickup and trailer. Back it up to the chute. I got a cow going to the sale in Bozeman!" He marched back out of the house mumbling to himself, "That old bat will think she won . . . until she sees herself laid out on a golden platter!"

Speaking from an outsider's point of view, I am just not real sure who won that contest! Thanks, Jim, for a good laugh—and just how many circles did you make around that corral?

On the other end of the state there was another animal story waiting for me. Actually a bird-in-the-hand story.

"Oh, honey, I think this is it," she cooed. As they flew by the house, they took another look. "The neighborhood is nice and there are trees and a beautiful garden."

"I like it too. Let's make it our home, the birthplace for our little ones," he chirped. So they did. They brought just the right sticks from near and far. In a few days they settled into their perfect nest. The human people who also live at that address, Gene and Kathy Ford, watched all the construction from their front steps. Before long the mother bird was sitting on several eggs in the well-built nest in the apple tree in the front yard. Daddy Bird was a faithful provider. When the eggs hatched, both Mommy and Daddy Bird were making "grocery trips." As the host family watched, they could see the little beaks pointed toward the sky awaiting the next feeding.

Kathy was sitting on the front step when it happened. One of the little baby birds ("Watch this, guys! I'll show you what I can do!") shakily perched on the edge of the nest . . . and fell right to the ground. Gene came running when he heard Kathy call. He saw the tiny little mop of wet downy feathers flap helpless little wings on the ground. The little bird hadn't passed flight training yet. A flat ground takeoff was impossible.

"The cat will get it if we don't do something," said Gene as he headed for the garage. He came back with a stepladder and leaned it against the tree. Then he went after the hapless little daredevil. The rescue effort was not without danger. Mommy and Daddy Bird came flying to the defense of their offspring when they heard the panicked chirping. Gene persevered. He carefully cupped his hand over the tiny fluttering baby. Navigating the rungs of the ladder and dodging the attacks of the dive-bombing parents, he bravely climbed. He set the fledgling pilot in the nest and climbed down the ladder.

He no sooner touched the ground than all four babies decided to jump. By now Kathy was part of the heroic effort. They chased the runaway infants and back up the ladder Gene went again with two of the babies. The parents were really agitated now. They did not understand the valiant recovery effort and the dangers of the cats on the ground. Their home and their family were under attack. They dove straight for the two-legged monster as he came down the ladder.

The Fords knew the little babies would soon be supper for the neighborhood cats. "Get a box," yelled Gene. Kathy ran into the house for a box. "Please, God, don't let the neighbors be watching," breathed Kathy as she raced to the basement. With athletic endeavor, the rest of the baby birds were captured and put in the box. With one hand holding onto the box and one hand holding onto the ladder, he again ascended the rungs to return the babies to their nest. John Audubon would have been proud. The four babies were returned to the nest despite the odds.

But the story doesn't end there. Unbelievably, before Gene could get the ladder back to the garage, the babies ("Let's do it again! That was fun!") jumped ship. Watching in utter disbelief as all four babies took the leap, Gene said, "That's it, I give up." Yet he felt honor-bound, and ducking the attacks of the panic-stricken parents, the newly formed Colstrip Chapter of Bird Baby EMTs rounded up the babies. They urged them over under a juniper bush by the front of the house. "They can spend the night there, " he told Kathy. "If they live, they live." He was out of breath from the rescue attempts.

There is a moral to this story, Kathy tells me. "One bird on the ground is better than four!"

The lady sat at the table in her kitchen in her home in Colstrip. She was making a list of the tasks to be accomplished this day so close to Christmas. Her granddaughter, a three-year-old moppet with big brown eyes, was busy playing with her toys on the floor.

"What ya doing, Gran'ma?"

"I'm making a list of what I have to do today."

"What ya gotta do, Gran'ma?"

"Well, first I have to go to the bank," the grandma said with a sigh.

Having heard the sigh, the toddler got up beside her grandmother and patted her knee, "That OK, Gran'ma, I go to food bank with you."

When this grandmother repeated this to me, the tears ran down her face. "It just breaks my heart to think the 'bank' to her is the 'food bank'—and to other kids, the bank is where you get money and lollipops." She was not making a judgment about the food bank. Both of us are so glad that this is available for those who need it. She was not making a judgment about her granddaughter's family. This little girl's daddy has been out of work for several months. He has tried to find work at every office and job site in the area and has worked at several short-term jobs. This grandmother's sorrow was focused on the fact that a place—the bank—accepted by the average family as the "money place" is the "food place" to others.

So it is with life's experiences. Each one of us faces the experiences that come into our lives differently.

One of my favorite people in this world is Bea Hawkins. She and her husband, Max, and their son, Bob, attend my folks' church, Emmanual Fellowship, in Livingston. She has been a faithful prayer-supporter of my ministry for several years. Recently we had the joy of visiting their home. It was so special. The Hawkins' home is filled to overflowing (even hanging from the ceiling) with antiques and treasures. It sits at the mouth of Paradise Valley and could be a museum. It is a testimony of the skill of seeing and acquiring the best of the best at garage sales and auctions through the years.

"The country look that so many decorators are trying to duplicate in pricey ways," I told my mom, who arranged the visit, "is supremely achieved in the Hawkins' home. But it is accomplished without a decorator and an expense account. It has happened with the love of history and perseverance."

We wandered from room to room, from artifacts to airplanes, to glassware and memorabilia, and then to the kitchen for a third cup of coffee. It is uniquely original and holds enough conversation pieces for lots of visits. "When we considered the price of carpet," Bea related, "we decided picking up carpet samples at 50 cents each was a much better buy. It turned out to be a wise decision. The first week after we attached all the pieces, our grandson spilled a bowl of chili. We just pulled up those two squares and replaced them!" And the creativity of putting together other pieces and parts has made an attractive and versatile home.

I like Max because he is a humble man. He was a pilot during the war and is very intelligent. But he is more excited about showing us his latest acquisition than elaborating his personal accomplishments.

Their son, Bob, is just like Forrest Gump. I would love to have him in my company. He remembers important things. Like people's names. And certain other things. (Lots of daily life stuff is not important for him to remember.) Bob came to the rescue when Max was helping a couple Sheetrock their home. The room was entirely Sheetrocked when someone said, in alarm, "Where was that electrical box? We covered it over!"

"Right over here," said Bob. Sure enough, when they cut the hole, there was the box!

"I have to tell you about my cleaning," Bea said. "I went to the cleaners in Livingston to pick up my cleaning. They couldn't find it. I was so distressed. They looked and looked. Finally I went out to the car. I was ready to cry. I needed those clothes!" She told me that she went back in a second time and asked them to look again. But still they couldn't find them.

"When I went back home, I was really upset," Bea said. "It was then that Bob said, 'Mom, that wasn't the cleaners. You took them to the other place!' He was right. I had to call the first cleaners and apologize. I am so glad for my 'special' son!"

Bob just beamed when Bea told this story. "I think I need to have your brain, Bob," I told him. "I keep remembering the unimportant stuff—and never remembering the important things!"

Maybe that is why Bea is one of my favorite people. She recognizes a gift from God. Thanks, Max, Bea and Bob. I think I heard the flutter of angel's wings when we were drinking coffee at your house, where God's abundant life is so evident!

"We call ours the clicker."

"We call ours the flipper."

"We call ours the flipper-dipper."

I said, "Well, we just call ours the remote."

You guessed it. It was a group of women discussing one of the hazards of marriage—the television remote control. It was unanimous.

Something happens to the male species when one of these little electronic devices gets in their possession. Remote *control* is an appropriate name. Place one of those little black boxes in the hand of a man and he becomes Zappo, Technical Controller of the Channels of the Universe. Maybe somewhere in our world there are a few exceptions. But in our discussion it was 100 percent.

"My husband says, 'Honey, come watch TV with me.' I put my book down and go to the living room. It's two minutes after the hour," says one woman. "He grabs the flipper-dipper. Click, we're watching a Western. I think, *Oh, this looks good,* and then click, it's a car chase. OK, this is fine. Click, sports. Click, music. Click, animals." She went on, "Finally he's asking me what I want to watch and it's fifteen minutes after the hour and we've missed the beginning of every show."

Sorry, men, but we all laughingly agreed. Soon the stories were going around the table. How frantic the Technician becomes when he can't find the remote. One lady said, "My husband said the reason he kept flipping through the channels is because that keeps recharging the batteries! I believed him!"

Another told of a neighbor who had to run to Billings (260 miles round trip) because his was lost for one day. Another said, "We solved that problem. My husband comes home from work and lies on the couch with *his* clicker at his side. I go in the bedroom and watch television in there with *my* remote." She went on, "Then about 10 o'clock, he comes to bed—and I get up and go lie on the couch—until he has checked out the channels in there a few more times—just in case they're different on the bedroom TV!"

But the best story of all and we'll never tell whose it was: "He" got up and prepared for work. The pencils and small calculator went in his shirt pocket and he was off. When "he" walked in the house after work he sank in his chair and grabbed for his remote control. He pointed it at the television and clicked and clicked and clicked. Nothing happened.

He looked down and couldn't believe it. He had his calculator in his hand!

It didn't take long for him, though. Without missing a beat, he laid the calculator back down on the end table by his chair. Then he reached in his pocket and slipped out the remote control—where it had ridden safe and secure in his pocket protector with him all day at work. What can I say? It must be in the genes!

Joseph was barely three feet tall. He wore daddy's shirt with a rope belt tied around his waist. Mary rode behind him on the donkey. The donkey was a tiny handcrafted wood wagon with a donkey's head, made of flannel and yarn, attached to the wagon. Two-year-old Mary rode in the wagon with serenity and complete trust in Joseph. Her dark brown hair and big brown eyes looked ahead to the cardboard stable. A talented artist had painted a contented cow and a fuzzy sheep amid the straw in the stable. A cardboard manger with a doll baby wobbled as Mary and Joseph took their places in the stable.

Flashbulbs sporadically brightened the stable scene as proud beaming parents and grandparents captured the precious moment for the future. As the age-old Christmas story was read from the second chapter of Luke, the shepherds and wise men stood waiting. "And there were in the same country shepherds abiding in the field, keeping watch over their flock by night " (Luke 2:8, KJV).

With a gentle nudge from their Sunday school teacher, the bathrobed shepherds started herding their flock down the aisle toward the stable. The two- and three-year-old "sheep" were clad in white long underwear with black socks on their feet and hands. Fuzzy white cotton ears and tails bobbed up and down as they crawled in front of the shepherds. "Baa, baa-a-a-a."

More flashes of brilliant light. A floodlight turned on from the balcony as the acting angel said, "Fear not, for behold, I bring you good tidings of great joy." Fourth- and fifth-grade carolers wrapped in coats and scarves echoed the refrain. Then three boys, who a few minutes before had been chasing each other around the church yard, walked regally down the aisle in satin robes with garlands of gold Christmas tinsel draped on their shoulders. Gold crowns rode precariously on their heads. The kings joined the sheep and shepherds at the stable. Blond-headed Joseph stood proudly under the cardboard stable roof. Little Mary smiled out in the crowd at Grandpa as she sat quietly by the manger.

A father concluded his reading, "And the child grew and waxed strong in spirit, filled with wisdom: and the grace of God was upon him." The congregation stood and sang "Silent Night."

The children collectively let out a sigh. The teachers sighed. The parents sighed. The director could breathe normally again. A few mothers dabbed their eyes with tissue. The Sunday school Christmas program at the Colstrip Alliance Church was over.

And so were hundreds of other Christmas programs across town and around the nation. In the midst of sometimes hectic holiday preparations filled with lists, parties and gift giving, attention was focused on the stable of Bethlehem and the babe in the manger—Jesus Christ, the greatest gift of all, who said, "I am come that they might have life, and that they might have it more abundantly" (John 10:10, KJV).

The spring snowstorm didn't dampen the spirit of Palm Sunday on March 31. Families spilled into the sanctuary for the early church service, mimicking the fall of huge snowflakes outside. However, one man said as he entered, "Can't quite get into the Easter mood. It is just too early this year." He took his seat in the pew with a slight frown on his face.

I didn't know with whom he was angry. Did he want the church to delay Easter until he was ready? Or did he want the calendar to wait for the daffodils? Or was the real reason deep within—his comment really a cry of his heart?

Other folks confessed a dire longing for the Easter service. Some of these were spiritually motivated. Others just wanted an end to winter coats and shoveling driveways. "Easter must bring spring," one woman mused. "It just has to!"

"Think back to Jerusalem," encouraged the worship leader as she began the service. I was already there. The ushers had handed palm fronds to each of us as we entered the service. Seeing the children waving them over their heads (of course, tapping brothers and sisters "accidentally" with their swings) took me whirling back to the streets of old.

*What a celebration it must have been that day,* I thought. Matthew records the events in detail in his Gospel. Palm branches and garments were thrown before Jesus as He wound through the streets. People were shouting "Hosanna! Hosanna!" and "Blessed is He who comes in the Name of the Lord!" Soon we twentieth-century worshipers were on our feet as well. Voices were lifted in praise and adoration pew by pew. The songs of redemption and forgiveness touched hearts, reminding each of us of what God has done in our lives. Then came songs of victory and triumph.

The frown was erased from the man across the aisle. The snow-weary woman had her hands lifted in praise. Rejoicing replaced the restlessness of discontent. Remembering anew Calvary's cross reenergized the joy of our salvation. One after another, worshipers made their way to the front to lay their palm fronds on the altar. A symbol of worship for the Lamb. An outward sign of an inner commitment.

It was hard for the children to part with the large green branch. Our four-year-old grandson, Justin, was beside me. "Justin, do you want to lay your palm branch up there for Jesus?" I whispered.

"No." It was a positive no! The dilemma was plain for him. If he took that thing up there, he would not be able to play with it any longer.

But a little boy across the church had solved that dilemma for himself. He raced to the front with one leaf from his palm frond. He placed it on the altar and zoomed back to his seat. A few moments later, he repeated the trip. And again. And again. Leaf by leaf. He didn't glance toward his parents who were on the platform leading the music. Their look might stop his repetitious sacrificial trips. When the branch was defrocked to a single green stem, the little boy sat contented in his seat. He had made it last longer than anyone else!

I was truly blessed by the Palm Sunday service and the sermon by the little boy touched me as deeply as the music and the "big people's sermon." Once again, I was reminded of the awesomeness of the Savior. He offers forgiveness and hope . . . but He allows us to come as we will. Some discouraged. Some weary. Some disillusioned. And some, leaf by leaf.

But to all He says, "I am the way, the truth, and the life: no man cometh unto the Father, but by me" (John 14:6, KJV). How we come to the cross varies. Crucial to us is that we come.

# CHAPTER 16

# Looking Back

I certainly am not the first person to realize that time changes things. I had the opportunity a few weeks ago to spend a summer morning riding the range with my folks. I was struck by the fact that time has changed so many of the things I grew up with.

The first thing I noticed was that horses are taller. I had a much more difficult time getting my foot in the stirrup and jumping up into the saddle. I think they are making saddles a lot smaller too.

As we rode up the creek to move some cattle, I spied The Falls. This was a favorite spot for my brother and me when we were kids. It was an adventure to pack a lunch and head for The Falls. The lake beneath The Falls was the subject of many major construction projects. Do you know that The Falls drop exactly thirty-two inches? And the little creek is smaller than its name of Buffalo Run? The pool at the bottom of the falls (I don't think I can capitalize them anymore since I have reexamined their geographical significance) is about four feet across. Worst of all—the falls are actually only a quarter of a mile from our ranch home! I would have sworn that it took my brother and me several hours to get there. Time sure changes things.

And the Big Hill. Another place to go for adventures. We'd always have to have all our chores done. We'd get our usual lecture on rattlesnakes from Mom. We'd pack a lunch. Then we'd either ride our horses or hike to the Big Hill. Rumor had it that two cowboys were buried up there. They had been killed in the early days by Indians. We were forever hauling rocks and making "monuments" to mark the "graves" every time we discovered the "actual" site. You could see all over the Shields Valley from on top the Big Hill. We became spies and lookouts and scouts from this vantage point.

Sad to say, the Big Hill has shrunk too and it is closer to the house than it used to be. I'm not sure you can even see all of the Shields Valley anymore.

The aging process is a weird thing, isn't it? I remember it used to take forever for a year, measured Christmas to Christmas, to get over. Now it seems a year is only six months long. Time goes faster while distances dwindle; my waist size gets bigger while creeks are getting smaller; and horses get taller and hills shrink. It is a weird thing.

"Please, please," we'd beg, "Can't we go to The Falls?" More often than not, my mother would relent. Ronnie, two years younger than myself, and I were often in the world of pretend. We were fortunate. Our world of pretend extended to the fence lines of the ranch. We played pretend with real horses. Naturally, that caused our folks some worries. We would fly across the fields shooting imaginary bullets at each other. We would set up camps in the creek bottoms where Wyatt Earp and Roy Rogers joined us for secret meetings. We were scouts for Lewis and Clark, covering the hills ahead of them, looking for buffalo. We hunted grizzly bears and fought ferocious Indian battles, the two of us, against all odds. We always won.

But of all the places, The Falls held the prime site of our pretend world. It was a great distance from our home and was close in spectacularness to the Upper Falls of the Yellowstone in Yellowstone

Park, seventy miles away. It took careful preparation to make a trip to the falls. We needed a lunch and always lugged a considerable number of favorite toys with us when we made a journey there. Though our trips encompassed many days in our imaginary world, the actual time was usually an afternoon.

We'd set up camp first. Then in short order, consume the lunch Mom had packed for us. What glorious times Ronnie and I had with our make-believe friends at our camp at the foot of The Falls! (I also remember the not-so-fun trips back up to the falls, when Mom discovered we hadn't brought any of our "stuff" back with us!)

On that recent ride past the falls, I shed not a few tears. Some of sadness, weeping over days never to be retrieved and lived again as carefree kids; some of thankfulness and a grateful heart to have had such a happy childhood. With a swipe of my hand, I wipe the tears away and rein my horse to catch up with Mom's. I see tears in her eyes too. Mom doesn't say anything. Neither do I. I know she knows. You can't go back. Just remember it, Lois. Like it was. And when you get an opportunity, share it with others.

We had a lilac hedge around the yard at the ranch. It must have been planted the same year the house was built in 1904 because they were big bushes. My little brother and I would play among them. It was hard to get between them and the fence because they were so thick. Of course, that made it a challenge—and a good hiding place.

My mom was never much of a flower person. She had a big garden, but it contained beans and beets and potatoes and corn—things that would be our groceries for the next winter. But in the spring of the year, she would start worrying if the lilacs would bloom. Those lilacs and a few of the tulips that grew in a spot in the backyard had to be ready by

Memorial Day. Getting flowers from a floral shop was unheard of in those days. My mom depended on those bushes to produce a living tribute of memory for those relatives who had "gone on before."

Memorial Day morning, Ronnie and I would go with her and help pick the fragrant lavender blossoms and put them in mayonnaise jars. (The Mason jars had to be saved for canning those beans.) It was my job to wrap aluminum foil around the jars to make them look pretty. It would be around 9:00 a.m. when we would all pile in the car with the lilacs and us sharing the back seat. First we would go to Livingston to the well-kept and carefully groomed cemetery there. It was fascinating for me to see all the little American flags blowing in the breeze beside the white markers "where soldiers are buried" I was told.

As long as I live, I will believe that the key words of visiting a cemetery are "Now just where is it?" My dad would say, "It's somewhere over there by that big pine tree," and we would be off in that direction. Then we'd find it. The Bohleen section. We would place a bouquet of lilacs on my Aunt Bessie's headstone and then stand back and look at it awhile. That part of the ritual I didn't understand then, but now I know it was the memorial tribute part. They were remembering.

Then back into the car and we would be on our way to Clyde Park, eighteen miles north. I always thought my mom must have lived in a "sadder" family because there were a lot of graves at Clyde Park that we put flowers on. The fact that "Dolly and her four babies" were buried there made an indelible impression on us kids. (It had something to do with that "Now I lay me down to sleep—if I should die before I wake" prayer, I think.) This cemetery didn't have mowed grass and big tombstones. There were no pine trees or rows of white markers and flags. Just little crosses and some flat markers. Here, before our silver and lavender arrangements could be placed, we would pull weeds. The cemetery phrase "Now just where is it?" wasn't necessary here. It was such a small place.

Then we'd do the stand-back-and-look-at-it thing. Then it was back into the car. We always, always had a family picnic gathering with other relatives in the afternoon. The picnic places varied, but the events of the day and their order never did change in all of my growing-up years.

So you can imagine my unbelief and shock when I heard my young (twenty-four-year-old) friend say when we were discussing three-day weekend plans, "Just where did the Memorial Day holiday come from, anyway?" I just thought everyone knew. In our family Memorial Day is still Memorial Day. Only now there are many new additions to our family plots. The Clyde Park cemetery has a caretaker now. There is green grass there. I think Dolly and her four babies would be pleased.

I am thankful I had the privilege of recording my Grandma Lennemann's life story before she went to heaven. Some of her story, about her faith in Jesus, how she lost her husband and her episode with smallpox, was written in *Breast Cancer and Me,* because she is part of my heritage and my spiritual foundation.

My maternal grandmother's parents were married in Benton, Iowa in 1877. They had their first baby in 1878. He lived not quite two weeks. Then they had Callie Bell, William Clyde, Ola Etta, Lawrence Ray, Richard Ernest, Thurman K., David Henry, Ethel Mae, Albert (he died shortly after birth), then Esther Fae and Elsie Neva and Joseph, who was stillborn. Then Lee John Victor. They left Iowa in 1903.

When asked why they left such rich country like Iowa to go to North Dakota, my great-grandmother said, "We heard about this free land up there. We could homestead 160 acres. All we had to do was live on it three years and build a house. Then it could be ours." There were twenty-three families from that vicinity that went. They called it an emigrant train. They took all their livestock, including six horses and some cows, their machinery and household goods.

Each family had a train car with their belongings. They had a coach for the women and children. The men went in with the livestock in a different train car. The length of the trip was about a week. They lived in a big tent twenty-three miles from Medina at first. They got their supplies from there. It took one day to go, a day to get the supplies and a day to return.

"One day my dad got caught in a blizzard and he was gone six days," my grandmother told me. "They didn't know where he was. They ran out of bread and flour. My mother told me that my brother would cry for bread." Grandma remembered lots about the North Dakota blizzards. She was born on November 24, 1905 in the midst of one. She was delivered by her mother and father.

In a blizzard, she told me, you could get lost going out to the pump in front of the house to get a bucket of water. They had a wire strung from the house to the barn so they could find their way. She said, "If there was even an empty nail hole in the house, it could almost fill the room with snow." They burned coal and cow chips for heat. There weren't any fences, so cattle had to be herded.

The blizzards were hazardous to livestock. One April in 1902, one rancher had twenty-five cows left after a three-day storm. He had lost ninety-two head. Another neighbor, her mother had told her, had eighteen survive out of 140 head. One had brought in 350 yearlings and had forty left. This disaster sent some back East and left dead livestock scattered over the North Dakota plains.

When we go through one of our Montana winters, I think back to my grandma and her parents. Then I thank God for my warm house and heat in my car, and I don't complain. It is not fair to my heritage.

My dad's family experienced severe weather problems also. I recently spent three days in Livingston. It was spring and the Yellowstone River was flooding. My aunt, Helen Bohleen Streblow, dug out a letter she had written after the flood of 1948. She was still living at my grandparents' ranch on the Shields River back then. It was so interesting that I asked her if I could share it with you. Not only is she a wonderful person, she is an artist and a writer. I think you will also appreciate her rendition of the event that follows.

## THE SHIELDS RIVER FLOOD—JUNE 1948

I don't know where to start this watery cyclone! Everything happened so fast that we didn't know what to do first. Friday the 4th was a lovely rainy day with a quiet but steady drizzle. It was doing the crops and the gardens a world of good. Andy and Bill drove cattle up to Goat Mountain and came home soaked. Pop was plowing up at the other place, and he was wet too when he came home. Mom and I worked at housecleaning and baking all day, as we planned on leaving for Billings for the Go Western Parade at 6 a.m. Saturday morning. We finished everything, including packing our suitcases. It was a good thing we did!

All day long we heard reports of this bridge and that one washing out. But still our own river here hadn't risen noticeably. That afternoon our neighbor got sick, and Bert [her fiancé she was to marry in September] and I took a thermometer up to him. On the way home we noticed the water was way up on the road. However, we weren't duly concerned and all retired early.

The next morning at 4:30 a.m., we heard Pop yelling up the stairs, "You boys better get up and take the cars out while it is still possible to get out." Everyone piled out. The boys had driven the six cars out by a quarter to 5. Mom and I were going from window to window looking at our old water marks from the first flood earlier this year. It seemed to be coming up so fast. When Andy drove Bill's Hudson out, he just made it. The water was already up past the running boards. We didn't eat breakfast until we had taken everything out that seemed necessary. Then the men noticed that the main channel right in the bend in the river was about to come across the road—in which case the house might be in danger.

Up to this point we hadn't worried about the house as it's on a high foundation, but the water was coming up so fast that we could expect anything. The boys started filling sandbags and hauling them in a trailer behind the Farmall tractor. In the meantime Mom and I were looking out the windows mostly. The big semi trailer had been up against the fence by the barn along with another horse trailer and other farm implements. We noticed the water up past the wheels on it.

I went out and took a movie of the nightmarish panorama. When I came back in the house I looked out again and the semi trailer was gone! It had floated down the channel between the house and the chicken houses but had hit a sandbar and stopped just before hitting the main channel of the river. We hoped it would stay there. Bud [Lois' dad] came in a few minutes later saying he would swim the channel for $600, which was what the trailer cost. He thought he could swim over and tie a rope from the trailer to a tree. However, while we were looking, it turned around a couple of times and then floated off down the river.

Just then one of the granaries (full of grain) moved about forty feet but stayed there for the time being. Too many things to watch! The next thing we saw was the rubber-tired wagon begin to tip. It had barrels of gas on it along with plowshares and some tools. One by one we saw them drop off and float down the river. The light pole was leaning against one of the chicken houses, so the men cut the power to the house. About 9:30 a.m., the men came in. Mom and I boarded a wagon with our suitcases and rode out to watch from the upper road. From there we saw the granary turn around a few times and go down the river. Soon after, the other one followed but got hung up on the same sandbar the trailer had been on. Also a binder, another wagon, the grinder and I don't know what all also went. A hayrack and the horse trailer floated down out of sight. The first granary hit a tree about a half mile from here and flew into a million pieces. Trees were falling all day long. I counted sixteen.

Well, the water got higher and the excitement was terrific. Lorraine [Lois' mom] and I made sandwiches. At 2:30 we noticed the chicken house had collapsed. It was a new building. The men were so busy that we took it on ourselves to call the sheriff. He said he would be right out with a boat. We met him at the road. They launched the boat, a ten-foot aluminum one, right at the mailbox. They asked for a man to go with the sheriff and the deputy, so Bert got in. They rowed peacefully until they came to the main channel and then—wow!

They lost an oar. They were grabbing every bush they came to. The water carried them on so fast it was hard to follow with our eyes. They hit the barn and Bert said he thought it would fall over them in pieces. But they got stopped at the first chicken house and filled eight or ten gunny sacks with chickens. Pop and Sonny threw a rope to them and kept one end themselves to tow the boat back.

The deputy, in his excitement, tied the rope to the wrong end of the boat, despite Bert and Pop yelling to him that it was wrong. When he let go of it, it turned over and the chickens went down the river! The deputy felt bad. He said it was all his fault. But when he stepped to the end of the boat, he unknowingly stepped into a five-foot hole that had been covered by a pump. (The pump had already gone down the river.) Guess he thought the river was plenty deep then! The men all laughed in spite of the tragedy. They did save about fifteen old hens from that coop. The river kept on rising until 5 in the afternoon. We all went over to Bud's and stayed a week. However, by the third day we could wade in. June 5 was Bud's birthday. He said if he celebrated it that way every year, it would be cheaper to knock him in the head!

Reading this story reminds me again that we all need to write down the things that happen in our lives. Though the brain forgets as we get older, if we write about experiences when they happen, they are recorded for future generations. Thanks, Aunt Helen, for letting me share this in another year of floods over fifty years later.

One of the joys of getting together with my family for holidays is the storytelling. Most of the stories are told every year. Those of us in the younger generation never get tired of them. As a matter of fact, we now add our own yarns to the family album, because there is a new generation behind us who need to learn. They need to learn the art of storytelling. And they need to learn the responsibility of passing these stories on.

The good thing about retelling the stories is with each telling we learn more details. Like with the window story. The Bohleens, Dad's family, settled in the Grass Range area of Montana in the early 1930s. In some way, my Grandpa Bohleen ended up with a horse-drawn hearse. It was an elegant thing. "We rode to school in style," said my Aunt Helen. "it was similar to a surrey but had a cab with windows." After a few years the elegant wagon was not in use.

When a neighbor was refurbishing an old cabin for his family, he came to my grandfather asking for some windows. Windows weren't easy to come by in those old days. "I can loan you the windows out of that old hearse," said my grandfather. So the man took the windows for his home. Years went by. The man and his family moved to another place, abandoning the cabin. "So we wanted the windows back. We were building a house and those windows were beautiful," said my Aunt Helen. "They were heavy beveled glass. Pa asked the man to return the borrowed windows before he left. But he wouldn't return them.

"Well, we were really angry. We wanted those windows back. So Ma, Bessie and I went to the County Attorney in Lewistown. He was very sympathetic with our plight. He didn't actually tell us to steal them back but he planted the idea with us!" Aunt Helen reported. "So that is just what we did. One day Bessie and I got on our horses and went after the windows."

"On horses?" I asked incredulously.

"Yes, we put some tools and a crowbar in a gunny sack and off we went. We didn't tell Ma or Pa where we were going. We just went." She said she went in the house and Bessie was on the outside being a lookout. "I was hot, I think I was so scared! In the process of getting the three windows out, they broke one. But they put the other two in the gunny sack and headed home. Bessie had to open all the gates because I was carrying the windows," Aunt Helen said. "When we got near the house, we knew we better hide the windows. Pa would not approve of his family being thieves no matter what the reason. So we found a grove of birch trees and carefully leaned the windows in a good hiding place. We never told anyone what we had done."

"Later in the week, I was out riding in the cow pasture," said my Uncle Sonny, picking up the story. "I saw the strangest thing. There was a bright light coming from one of the gullies. I rode over to see what it was. The sun was just right and the light was a brilliant reflection of the sun . . . on the windows. I did not tell anyone what I saw."

Later in the year the family moved to another place. All their belongings were packed on wagons. A large, carefully wrapped box was tied to the top of their car. My grandfather just smiled when everyone questioned what was in the box. "I think you all know," he said. "You just did not know that I knew. It is the windows."

So somewhere in central Montana, probably in the falling-down ruins of an old house, is part of my family heritage. The windows.

I guess you know one of the things we have planned for next summer. Robert and I are going on a treasure hunt. We just won't ride horses!

In my family, it is hard to capture the true color of the storytelling at family dinners with pen and ink. For one thing, the pen could never record the interruptions necessary for the story to be told right, no matter who the storyteller is. One of my favorites from the 1920s, that each of my aunt and uncles who still are living loves to tell, is about their brief foray into the magazine-selling business.

Grandma Bohleen had lain down for a few minutes of well-earned rest, which she needed as a young mother of four. Her brood was out under a tree in the front yard when she dozed off. Soon Helen and Lillian thought of a brilliant money-making idea. They would sell *Farmer's Wife* magazines around the area. Lillian, at the ripe old age of nine, was selected as driver. The four kids ran to Grandpa's big old Buick and took off down the road. They wheeled out of the yard, zooming down the country roads.

At the first place, they got strange looks over the age of the car's occupants and a refusal for *Farmer's Wife*. At the next place, a post got in the way of their turn into the farmer's gate. But Lillian, so Uncle Sonny tells it, gallantly drove over the top of it and pulled up in front of the house with finesse. No one was home.

One of the houses was at the bottom of a curve going down a hill. Lillian didn't have a whole lot of experience with driving or operating a gear shift, but with shrieks and howls, they made it around the corner and down the hill. They sold two subscriptions on their entire trip (which they never sent into the magazine, they sheepishly related—and still feel guilty about seventy years later). They recollected that the money they made must have been spent on gas.

Needless to say, Grandma was up from her nap when they got home. She was so glad to see the salespeople and the car in one piece that their punishment was not too severe. Anyway, how can you ground four kids and tell them they can't drive for a week when they are all under the age of nine?

My mom remembers a Christmas many years ago as one of her favorite memories. "It was a grab-bag Christmas," she told me. "We were each given a dime to buy a gift that would go in a box. Then each member of our family would get to draw one gift out for themselves. Even more than the gifts, I remember Mom sending us all out of the living room for some time. She closed the door. When she said we could come back in, there was a big surprise.

"Mom had purchased, with her egg money, candles with special little holders for the tree. She lit the candles. We got to stare at it in wonder for ten minutes. Then she blew out the candles. It was the prettiest tree I can ever remember."

The foundation is the most important component of any building, whether it is a garden shed or a high-rise office building. The same principles apply to us. How we react to life is determined by what kind of foundation we have.

What if the foundation in my life is built on my athletic endeavors and abilities, and an injury prevents further pursuit of sports activity? Or if my foundation is built on my looks, what happens one morning when I look in the mirror and see wrinkles and sagging skin? Or in my profession, what happens when I lose my job? What if we build all our hopes and dreams on our spouse or another person and he or she fails to meet our expectations?

People build their lives on many different foundations: their abilities, their possessions, performance of their children, their church affiliation, the assurance of money in the bank—or even being thin, popular or having the best house in the neighborhood. Do you notice something about all of these? They can fade away or be lost or destroyed.

My foundation, a rich heritage of a wonderful family and parents who love me, is important to who I am. As much as that has contributed to my life, it is not enough to guarantee a happy, fulfilled life for me. Just take into consideration how many others have the same or similar heritages and are unhappy, miserable human beings.

A foundation built on the Lord Jesus Christ is everlasting. The faith of my ancestors, as real as it was and is for them, cannot be passed on to their descendants automatically. I, and my generation, must make it our own. God says in His Word,

> My sheep hear my voice, and I know them, and they follow me: And I give unto them eternal life; and they shall never perish, neither shall any man pluck them out of my hand. My Father, which gave them me, is greater than all; and no man is able to pluck them out of my Father's hand. (John 10:27-29, KJV)

Each one of us must answer the Shepherd's call for his own life.

The times we are living through are confusing. They are much different times than those of my grandparents, my aunts and uncles, and my folks. News reports and happenings in lives around us can shake our security and sense of well-being. Things are not the way they used to be and what they used to be was not all perfect either. I heard one person say, "Who can you trust anymore?"

That part of life has not changed since the times of my grandparents and those generations before them. The same choice remains for each of us. *We can trust God.* I know by personal experience that His Word is true and He is who He says He is. We can have the assurance that our lives are built on a solid rock foundation by choosing to follow Jesus Christ.

"For no one can lay any foundation other than the one already laid, which is Jesus Christ," God said plainly (1 Corinthians 3:11).

There are two things you need to know before we end this chapter: 1. God is willing to come into your life, forgive your sin and give you that most abundant life. John 3:16 says, "For God so loved the world, that he gave his only begotten Son, that whosoever [that includes you] believeth [puts his trust] in him should not perish, but have everlasting life" (KJV).

2. Maybe you did not have the love and support of a caring family such as I have described. My word to you is this: "A new heritage can start with you. Trust God with your life. Then let the blessings pass on from you to others in your family and the next generations."

I will be praying that you make that decision to trust God for the foundation of your life this day.

# CHAPTER 17

# And Now . . .

Mom and Dad will celebrate their sixtieth wedding anniversary on September 24, 2001. It is hard to believe. They can work circles around the rest of us and look much younger too! I know how blessed I am to have my parents living close enough that we can see each other often. Many times they drive 100 miles east to Billings, we drive 130 miles west to Billings, and we meet to spend the day together. Many of my friends do not have that same privilege. That has taught me to appreciate each day we can spend together.

They have been an example to the rest of us on partnership in a marriage. Never were there "her" jobs and "his" jobs. They share ranching together. My mom is as ready to help Dad fix a fence as he is to share in cooking a meal (or making toast!). Although she says he still can't run a washing machine and she doesn't ever irrigate, they share each day's work together.

Each morning is started with a pot of coffee. Mom gets it all set the night before. Then Dad gets up early (sometimes very early) in the morning, starts a fire and plugs the coffee in when he hears Mom stirring back in the bedroom. Dad will read *Our Daily Bread* and the Bible verses that go with it. Usually the phone starts ringing about 5:30 a.m. It might be Uncle Sonny, Dad's brother, or Calvin, my cousin. If it's Calvin, they'll discuss cow prices and market trends. If it's Uncle

Sonny, they'll talk about old times and who sold that gray mare to whom, who used to live on the old Sweeny place and other stuff, ending with cow prices and the hay market and what they will be doing for the day. By then Mom has her coffee and is in her chair on the other side of the woodstove in the living room of their log house.

I must mention the coffee. Dad has one of those old white ceramic mugs that is at least half an inch thick. He first pours hot water in it to "warm it up." Every morning. Then he gets Mom's brown mug, a newer one with flowers on it that my Aunt Doris gave her, and pours hot water in it. Every morning.

When I'm at the ranch, he fills my white mug with the pink cancer ribbon on it full of hot water also. I always have to sneak a little cold water into my coffee when he isn't looking because I like mine a little cooler. They take turns getting up to fill each other's coffee cups until the pot is just about empty.

During this time, my brother has probably called from Big Piney, Wyoming. I usually make my call a little after 7. The radio will be on. They will listen to John Polaski's weather report and the local news or a market report. Then they shut the radio off, because it is prayer time. Every morning they pray for us, the grandkids and the great-grandkids, naming each one and praying specifically for what is going on in their lives. They pray for friends and relatives, their pastor and church, and for folks with problems. They always thank God for the blessings He has bestowed on them.

Then it's time for breakfast. Mom decides the menu (Dad gets eggs and bacon twice a week by her decree!). Dad makes the toast. Dad always says grace for breakfast. Then they get on with their day. In the evening, sometimes late, sometimes earlier, they finish supper and are in their chairs on each side of the woodstove again. More than likely, they will put in a Gaither Homecoming video to watch. (One of the highlights of our lives was driving the 600 miles to Denver, Colorado together to see their Homecoming Friends and meeting Jake Hess, their favorite, in person two years ago.)

Then the evening phone calls come from the grandkids, scattered through various states. Although they don't each call every night, they all call at least once a week. Papa and Gram are never too busy to talk to their grandkids and/or to chat with one of those five great-grandkids. They watch the 10 o'clock news and check the weather report for the next day. Then they walk down the hall to go to bed, shutting off the lights, with Mom always saying, "Did you put a log in the stove?" and Dad saying, "Yup. Did you make the coffee?" and Mom saying, "Yup." and then Dad saying, "I guess we can go to bed then."

We are all blessed by my parents. An indication of how much we want to model their marriage for our own is evident in our choice of wedding days. Robert and I were married on September 15, Todd and Lisa on September 28, Kevin and Kelli on September 14, and Ross and Melissa on October 3. (They were getting married at the ranch and the September dates were all filled.) So each September we have a grand month of honoring the marriages in our family and especially the anniversary of Bud and Lorraine Bohleen, whom we so appreciate and love. We appreciate their prayers, their inspiration and their faith that carry over into each of our families. You don't have to tell us we are "lucky."

We know it. And we know it isn't luck.

After celebrating our anniversaries in September, our next annual traditional get-together is Thanksgiving. This year, a special molded green salad was to be my contribution for the dinner. No one could distract me as I prepared my dish in Mom's kitchen. Even though my family knows my cooking reputation, I was determined to knock their socks off with my salad.

Thanksgiving dinner is held at my Uncle Sonny's ranch up Paradise Valley, west of Livingston. His home was built long ago and bulges at the seams as aunts and uncles, cousins, kids and friends arrive. This year he told us he had spent three days cleaning his house before we came, and even though it isn't his favorite chore, he said, "It's the getting started that's hard. After that, it isn't too bad."

We thought he must have even polished his famous old coffeepot in which he makes the stoutest cowboy coffee known! When we "girls" arrived, we spread out the dining room table, added one other table at the end that Sonny had found at a second-hand store (just for his entertaining) and spread the tablecloths. The dinner china, green and gold-rimmed, bordered with pastel flowers, was my Grandma Bohleen's, and it makes the table set for twenty so festive.

Uncle Bert cooks the turkey, Aunt Helen makes the gravy, my dad does the spuds and his famous scalloped-corn dish. Cousin Susan continues family traditions with her mom's scalloped oysters. Suze did a ham up royal this year with a berry glaze that looked like it came out of a magazine. There was Aunt Lillian's baked sweet potatoes. She's gone now, but by following her recipe out of our family cookbook, we did OK. Others brought pies, salads, vegetable dishes and relish trays, proving to us that they could cook also.

Finally everyone had arrived, and the food, including my green molded salad, covered every inch of the stretched-out table. We held hands as we thanked the Lord for His blessings upon the family members who couldn't be with us and prayed for those in our world less fortunate than we.

Before the dishes had made one pass around the table, my plate was full. I couldn't help checking the progress of my salad. I have had the experience so often of taking something to a potluck and having most of it left. (Robert says people are starting to know my pans and dishes!)

Conversation covered the gamut of the prices of calves and wheat, news of the younger ones in the family scattered across the country, and who was going and not going to the National Rodeo Finals next week in Las Vegas.

When Uncle Sonny asked for thirds of the green molded salad, I couldn't help myself. "Who made that salad?" I asked.

"I don't know," he said.

"Why don't you ask?" I said.

"OK," he said. "Who made this salad?"

"I did," I said.

"It's good," he said with a smile.

Now I am back home, sitting at my desk, adding another item on my thankful list in my journal. I stop to pray, "Dear Lord, I am thankful that You don't strike me down when my pride jumps ahead of me. I really am sorry. I just couldn't help it . . . that salad was really good! You know, Lord, maybe if You granted me more success in the kitchen, I could be a lot more humble. Amen."

I want to end this book with four of my favorite things. First my most favorite psalm:

PSALM 100

Make a joyful noise unto the LORD, all ye lands.
Serve the LORD with gladness: come before his presence
      with singing.
Know ye that the LORD he is God:
it is he that hath made us, and not we ourselves;
we are his people, and the sheep of his pasture.

Enter into his gates with thanksgiving, and into his
    courts with praise:
be thankful unto him, and bless his name.
For the LORD is good; his mercy is everlasting;
and his truth endureth to all generations. (KJV)

And my most favorite column:

Four conversations were going on at once. The interior of the car was
filled to capacity with my friends and the baggage that could not be
stuffed into the full trunk. Excitement was at a peak. We were going to
a ladies' retreat. No cooking. No husbands or children. A three-day escape from reality. A ladies-only slumber party.

I put the key in the ignition and said, "Let's pray before we take off."
I could see the ladies in the other two cars were doing the same.

As we bowed our heads, the designated pray-er said, "Lord, we ask
You to watch over our husbands and children until we return. In Jesus'
name, amen." I pulled out of the parking lot following the other two
cars.

First there was a little giggle, then a snicker and soon the whole car
full of women was laughing uproariously. From the backseat someone
caught her breath and said, "Oh, isn't that just like us? Did you hear
what she said?" Then followed more uncontrollable laughter.

Yup. Just like us. "Dear Lord, please take care of things until *we* get
back . . . then *we'll* take over again!"

In talking with a friend this week about a future goal in his life, he
said, "I am leaving a space open for God to show me His direction in
this . . . " Then he smiled. "That was certainly a play on words, wasn't
it? *I'm* leaving a space open for God."

It is in us from the top of our heads to the tips of our toes: we must be in control. We, the created, "allow" the Creator to interface in our lives. So humble of us, right? It is like going to the car lot and picking out a new car. Then saying, "OK, God, I'll let You pick the color." Then going home feeling so sanctimonious because we "let" God have a part in the decision.

Maybe you never have this problem. But I do. Often. Mostly because I am in a hurry and don't want to wait on God for a decision. Or because I really don't think He will give me the answer I want. So my prayer goes like this: "Dear Lord, here's what I want to do. Bless it, OK?"

I am reminded again of the story in the Bible about the Potter and the clay. I get a visual picture of the little clay pot with its hands on its sides telling the Potter, "Now here's the way you're going to make me!"

On my desk I have a copy of a prayer given for the National Prayer Breakfast one year by Kay Coles James, an aide at the White House:

Father, thank You that in You our pasts are redeemed, our present makes sense, our future is secure . . . Fill us with Your Spirit so that we don't have to be right, first, tops, recognized, praised, regarded, or rewarded. Help us to live by faith, lean on Your presence, walk by patience, lift by prayer and *labor by Your Power.* Amen.

And "Amen"!

My other most favorite column:

Over Labor Day weekend, the man whom with I will soon celebrate forty years of marriage and I went to our mountain hideaway in the Big Horn Mountains in Wyoming. The next two months were scheduled full with speaking engagements and writing responsibilities. I need to rest and prepare for a busy eight weeks. The beautiful mountains, cool, crisp air and the sound of the creek running nearby was a haven of rest. We sat, we read, we played games and took a trip exploring every morning. In the evening, we always drive down lower in the valley to see the moose and elk grazing contentedly.

I was studying the 23rd Psalm, sitting in a lawn chair out under a pine tree. That is when I saw something new in the old favorite psalm. Recite it with me:

> The LORD is my shepherd; I shall not want. He maketh me to lie down in green pastures: he leadeth me beside the still waters. . . .

Whoa! Stop! He maketh me to lie down in green pastures? He *maketh* me to lie down? Now why would He have to "maketh me"? Do you suppose because I won't want to do it on my own? That I might just keep postponing rest until I forget it altogether? That resting doesn't come naturally to many of us? So since it is necessary, according to our Shepherd, we may find ourselves being herded into the sheepfold for a little R and R when He thinks we need it.

My eyes stopped at that next line, "He leadeth me." Why do we lead something? Because "it" won't follow of its own accord. That brought images of the Park County Fair in about 1958 and my being dragged around the fairgrounds arena by my 4-H steer. I looked good too in my white shirt and green string tie. I know that from the home movies my mom took. You can also tell that two weeks before the fair wasn't soon enough to start breaking this big hunk of beef to lead.

I wondered, as I sat there, if sometimes God feels that I am a runaway sheep. That it is necessary to put the halter on and lead Lois by the still waters? I went on through the psalm, verse by verse, enlightened by the Holy Spirit into new understanding of each verse and seeing how it applied to my life, right now, right here, right where I am.

It was nearly two hours later when I needed to pray. Before I could do that, I pulled my jacket around my shoulders. There was a cool breeze. Then I bent my head while chipmunks chattered in the treetops. "Lord, today I see so many new things in this psalm. I am so grateful that You do not give up on me. Forgive me for my busyness and my unwillingness to be led by You so many times. Thank You for all the ways You have led me in the past and the green pastures You provided for me. I am so grateful we have a place to come and rest and study Your Word. I want to be a faithful sheep. In Jesus' name, amen."

"Do you want to take a little ride?" Robert asked as he laid his book aside.

"Sure," I said. "I'll just put my Bible in the trailer."

He headed the pickup west to Burgess Junction near the top of the pass and then suddenly slowed down. "Wow, look at that!"

Crossing the road in front of us were several bands of sheep. Hundreds of sheep. A sheep wagon was being pulled by a pickup. Several guys were helping flag traffic and move the sheep safely across the road. The sheepherder and his dogs were off to one side guiding the sheep through a gate. We watched the scene in front of us for several minutes.

"You OK?" Robert asked as he heard me blowing my nose and saw me wiping the tears from my face.

"Yup, I am fine. Just a little lesson God was teaching me . . . I didn't know He was going to illustrate the lesson in living color right before my eyes. Of course, that is just like our Lord, isn't it? Our Shepherd."

My other most favorite psalm:

PSALM 23

The LORD is my shepherd; I shall not want.
He maketh me to lie down in green pastures:
> he leadeth me beside the still waters.
He restoreth my soul:
he leadeth me in the paths of righteousness for his name's sake.
Yea, though I walk through the valley of the shadow of death,
> I will fear no evil:
for thou art with me; thy rod and thy staff they comfort me.
Thou preparest a table before me in the presence of
> mine enemies:
thou annointest my head with oil; my cup runneth over.
Surely goodness and mercy shall follow me all the days
> of my life:
and I will dwell in the house of the LORD for ever. (KJV)

Jesus said, *"I am come that they might have life, and that they might have it more abundantly." (John 10:10, KJV)*

AFTERGLOW

In my book *Breast Cancer and Me,* published by Christian Publications, Inc., I gave testimony to the love and support and encouragement that I receive from my best friend and husband, Robert. I am so blessed to be married to him. In this book I wanted readers to meet my parents to let you know how blessed I feel being their daughter. I thank God that I was raised in a Christian home and that my parents and others in my family continue to be an inspiration to me.

On the day the first copy of *Breast Cancer and Me* was delivered to our house in the mail, I was so excited I could hardly contain myself. Our grandson Justin happened to be at our house. I said, "Look Justin, here is Grammi's book. The one I have been working on and telling you about. It's done!" He took it in his hands, looked at the front cover, turned it over, looked at the back cover and then handed it back to me, saying, "Now, can you write one about me?"

So maybe that is where God will lead next—a book about our kids and their kids. As soon as we think we are done raising them—I'll get right on it!

Thank you for reading this book. God bless,

Lois (the Dude)

To contact Lois about a speaking engagement,
write to her at

## P.O. Box 907
## Colstrip, Montana 59323

or e-mail her at

## olmstead@mcn.net

## Also look for these other titles by Lois Olmstead:

*Breast Cancer and Me*
*Enjoying the Journey*
*Denim and Lace* (with Phyllis Rowe)